# water-smart
# GARDENING

Quarto is the authority on a wide range of topics.

Quarto educates, entertains and enriches the lives of our readers—enthusiasts and lovers of hands-on living.

www.quartoknows.com

First published in 2015 by Cool Springs Press, an imprint of Quarto Publishing Group USA Inc., 400 First Avenue North, Suite 400, Minneapolis, MN 55401 USA. Telephone: (612) 344-8100 Fax: (612) 344-8692

quartoknows.com
Visit our blogs at quartoknows.com

Cool Springs Press titles are also available at discounts in bulk quantity for industrial or sales-promotional use. For details contact the Special Sales Manager at Quarto Publishing Group USA Inc., 400 First Avenue North, Suite 400, Minneapolis, MN 55401 USA.

10 9 8 7 6 5 4 3 2 1

ISBN: 978-1-59186-644-2

Library of Congress Cataloging-in-Publication Data
Names: Maranhao, Diana, author.
Title: Water-smart gardening : save money, save water, and grow the garden you want / Diana Maranhao.
Description: Minneapolis, MN : Cool Springs Press, 2016. | Includes index.
Identifiers: LCCN 2015025392 | ISBN 9781591866442 (pb)
Subjects: LCSH: Xeriscaping. | Drought-tolerant plants. | Water conservation.
Classification: LCC SB475.83 .M32 2016 | DDC 635.9--dc23
LC record available at http://lccn.loc.gov/2015025392

Acquiring Editor: Billie Brownell
Project Manager: Alyssa Bluhm
Art Director: Brad Springer
Cover Designer: Amy Sly
Layout: Diana Boger

# water-smart
# GARDENING

**save water, save money, and grow the garden you want**

DIANA MARANHAO

Cool
Springs
Press
*Home and Garden Experts™*

*This book is dedicated to my son Steve, daughter Destiny, and to my husband Steve, my biggest supporters throughout my life and horticulture career; to my friends, who "get" what I am about; and to the horticulture industry, which shares in the stewardship of the land and the goal of "keeping the green."*

# Acknowledgments

So many people have contributed to the making of this book that it is difficult to give the credit that they deserve. First of all, thank you Billie Brownell, of Quarto US/Cool Springs Press, for all your efforts to launch the idea for the book, pursuing its approval, choosing me for its author, and for your guidance in writing it. Brad Springer patiently answered my questions about the art process. Tracy Stanley and Alyssa Bluhm gently guided me through the computer speak of uploading, downloading, saving, and sharing files.

I want to acknowledge everyone who played a part in the making of *Water-Smart Gardening*. You shared the vision, gave me counsel, and helped bring my words to life.

· For bringing clarity to my thoughts through your brilliant illustrations: Jeri Deneen and Jon Powell of Deneen Powell Atelier, Inc.

· For your tireless efforts in supplying images of your work of beautiful landscapes that bring xeric garden design to new levels, Steve Harbour of Steve Harbour Landscapes.

· For sharing images of your work, Ryan Prange of Falling Waters Landscape and Mary Evans of Prairie Nursery, Inc.

· For photos of beautiful demonstration gardens and your efforts in continuing education in water conservation and sustainability, John Bolthouse, Jan Tubiolo, and Pam Meisner of The Water Conservation Garden, Calif., and Linda Townes of Conservation Garden Park, Utah.

· For sharing your expertise, insights, and images: Steve Maranhao, Elim Valley Nursery; Loa LaDene and Sheri Meyerholtz; Helen M. Stone, *Southwest Trees & Turf*; Rose Epperson, West Coast Arborists, Inc.; Brad Monroe, Cuyamaca College; Bill Millward and Maureen Nassie, Netafim USA; Victor Vargas, Rain Bird; Chris Roesink, Hunter Industries; Enrique Moran and Vana Ankeny, Toro; Alice Newton and Christie Vanover, National Park Service/Lake Mead; Dawn Barraclough, Springs Preserve; Melissa Meyers; ML Robinson, University of Nevada Cooperative Extension.

# Contents

# Everybody Talks about Drought but Nobody Does Anything about It

**W**E CAN HARDLY avoid the issue of water. It would seem every time we watch the news, drought, dwindling water resources, and rising water costs are making the headlines. Almost daily, there are images of parched landscapes and dropping water levels in lakes and reservoirs, accompanied by the news that there is no rainfall on the horizon, we must conserve water, and we can expect our water bills to dramatically increase.

In water-taxed regions, gardeners constantly deal with water-supply issues, so water rationing and conservation is the norm. On the other hand, there are some areas that have no water restrictions in place. They use water in abundance, with impact sprinklers running all night watering fields of weeds, with the attitude of, "If you don't use it, you lose it." And then there is the haphazard waste of water. We have all seen sprinklers running midday, water escaping down the street, and landscapes with park-like expanses of turf. Everyone seems to be talking about drought and strained water resources, but no one seems to be doing anything about it.

Water issues affect everyone nationwide. In addition to the concern for our most precious natural resource, the cost of water affects us all, whether we pay more to keep our gardens green or at the market to keep our families fed. Short- and long-term droughts, a national decline in water resources, construction of pipelines and storage systems, and repairing antiquated infrastructures all contribute to rising costs of water. The bad news: it's likely to get worse before it gets better.

---

**After a monsoon rain, the landscape gets a good soaking. The irrigation systems can be turned off for a week, but in the triple-digit heat of summer, the reprieve from watering is short-lived.**

7

**Water is our most precious natural resource. Water-smart gardening makes every drop count.**

The *good* news is that you can learn to garden with what you have in a more resource-conscious way.

*Water-Smart Gardening* brings some tried-and-true garden practices back to the limelight, such as zonal plantings—a new term that addresses the age-old practice of companion gardening. Directing the flow of water with earthworks such as terraces, berms, and contours uses soil and water conservation practices from long ago. Rainwater harvesting allows you to harness the rain and use it where and when you need it, which is as simple as placing a bucket under an eave, or capturing as much of the rain or snowfall as possible by installing a water-storage cistern catchment system.

"Water-Wise Watering" (Chapter 4) offers user-friendly irrigation system design options that use low volume sprinklers and drip/micro-water emitters to apply water slowly and deeply to a plant's roots where it is needed. New methods and technology in "Water-Conserving Solutions" (Chapter 5) will help you manage soils for better water movement and nutrient absorption. Select water-thrifty native plants and those that come from other arid regions to fit into your design style. *Water-Smart Gardening* will show you how to create healthy gardens while conserving water by gardening the water-smart way. We will talk about drought, and we *will* do something about it!

# Water Challenges & Changing Landscapes

We are known for our arid climates throughout the Southwest, where I live, yet in some years we are blessed with monsoons. Temperatures climb to triple digits for days on end, clouds finally begin to form, and within an hour's time, thunder claps loudly and lightning flashes, illuminating the darkened skies and bringing forth torrential rain. Considered a "good gully washer" by farmers and gardeners in our valley, the rain gives some relief. But we are always preparing for dry spells and drought, knowing that the monsoons are just a temporary reprieve.

Precipitation maps, monitored and recorded by the National Weather Service, show average amounts of rainfall we can expect to receive in a year. Rainfall maps are compiled from years of data, so averages will encompass years of high amounts of precipitation and years of less than normal amounts. The map gives gardeners a starting point of what might be expected for rainfall, and that information is helpful for matching plants to the environment that will support them.

The USDA Cold Hardiness map, developed and updated by the U.S. Department of Agriculture, notes the coldest winter temperatures on record *on average* for the United States, and divides the nation into hardiness zones based upon the lowest average temperature ranges. Knowing the USDA Zone for your area helps you select plants that can survive even the coldest winter temps. If you are on the boundary of two intersecting zones, then choose the colder zone as your guide, giving your plants the added assurance of survival. For example, where I live, the USDA Zone map designation is Zone 6 (-10 to 0 degrees Fahrenheit). However, the little farm I share with my husband is out of town by just 11 miles but it is 1,000 feet higher in elevation. We decided to use Zone 5 ( 20 to -10 degrees Fahrenheit) as our guide. Our losses due to cold temperatures have been minimal, especially for the trees and shrubs that are the largest investment in time and resources and the foundation of a landscape.

# Drought, Dwindling Water Resources & Strained Water Budgets

By definition, drought is a period of prolonged dryness that causes extreme damage to plants or prevents them from developing successfully. It means different things in different areas of the country. A short-term drought may be used to describe lack of rainfall for just a matter of months in Florida, where the state receives an annual average of 54 inches of rainfall. Extreme drought conditions can persist for years in California when it does not receive the statewide average of 22 inches of rainfall per year.

Droughts have occurred throughout history, the most notable being the Dust Bowl years in the 1930s. From 1934 to 1940, this drought affected over 70 percent of the nation, starting in the Southwest, then spreading to the Great Plains. The devastating effects of the Dust Bowl era were long-lasting due to overtillage of farmlands, which led to severe soil erosion. The Heartland, which provided agricultural crops and products for the nation, was plagued with long-lasting effects of crop loss, depleted soil tilth, and disease and pests that followed in the aftermath. Some of the positive aspects that came out of the Dust Bowl era were in the research, restoration, and soil conservation efforts.

From 1951 to 1956, yet another drought affected the Great Plains and eventually

## USDA plant hardiness zone map

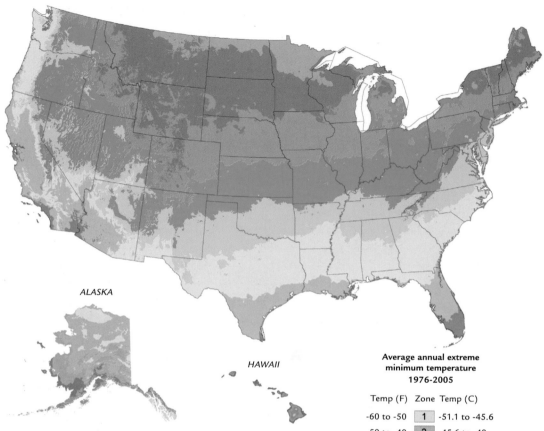

ALASKA

HAWAII

Find your location as closely as you can on the map and note the corresponding cold hardiness zone. If your location intersects with two zones, then use the colder winter temps/zone as your guide to select plants for your garden.

**Average annual extreme minimum temperature 1976-2005**

| Temp (F) | Zone | Temp (C) |
|---|---|---|
| -60 to -50 | 1 | -51.1 to -45.6 |
| -50 to -40 | 2 | -45.6 to -40 |
| -40 to -30 | 3 | -40 to -34.4 |
| -30 to -20 | 4 | -34.4 to -28.9 |
| -20 to -10 | 5 | -28.9 to -23.3 |
| -10 to 0 | 6 | -23.3 to -17.8 |
| 0 to 10 | 7 | -17.8 to -12.2 |
| 10 to 20 | 8 | -12.2 to -6.7 |
| 20 to 30 | 9 | -6.7 to -1.1 |
| 30 to 40 | 10 | -1.1 to 4.4 |
| 40 to 50 | 11 | 4.4 to 10 |
| 50 to 60 | 12 | 10 to 15.6 |
| 60 to 70 | 13 | 15.6 to 21.1 |

Source: Agricultural Research Service, U.S. Department of Agriculture; The PRISM Climate Group, Oregon State University

encompassed a ten-state region. In the first year of the drought, Texas' annual precipitation rate dropped by 40 percent, while temperatures remained in the triple digits, which led the federal government to declare Texas a drought disaster region.

A short, two-year drought, from 1987 to 1989, eventually affected 36 percent of the nation. This drought had the highest economic impact on record, with losses in agriculture, water, and energy resources. Widespread fires followed the drought's path.

The most recent drought index (at the time of writing this book) shows that nearly 40 percent of the U.S. is in the midst of drought or will be in the next few years. According to the National Integrated Drought Information System (NIDIS), the U.S. Drought Monitor (September 23, 2014) shows almost the entire state of California and portions of Texas and Oklahoma are in exceptional drought conditions. The remaining parts of California,

**Mean annual precipitation, 1981-2010**

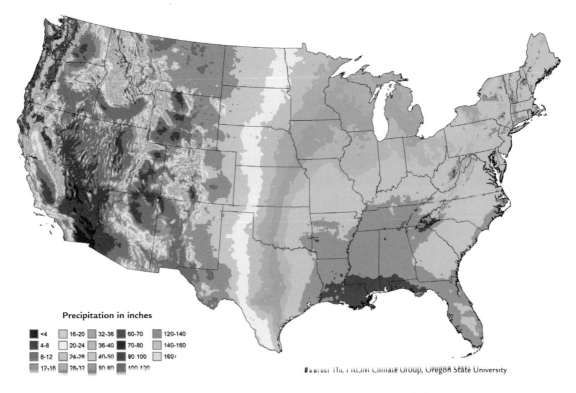

Precipitation in inches

| | |
|---|---|
| ■ <4 | □ 16-20 |
| ■ 4-8 | 20-24 |
| ■ 8-12 | 24-28 |
| 12-16 | 28-32 |

32-36 · 36-40 · 40-50 · 50-60 · 60-70 · 70-80 · 90-100 · 100-120 · 120-140 · 140-160 · 160+

Source: The PRISM Climate Group, Oregon State University

This precipitation map gives gardeners an estimate of how much rain or snowfall they might see on average for the year.

almost two-thirds of Oregon, the western portion of Nevada, southern Idaho, and Arizona are experiencing extreme drought. Severe drought conditions are prevalent in central Washington, Idaho, and the Southwestern states. Moderate droughts and abnormally dry conditions exist across the U.S., in typically high rainfall areas of the South, and all the way up the Eastern Seaboard.

Droughts have occurred throughout climate history and have a tendency to return to the same areas. In some regions, years of meeting or exceeding average rainfall amounts become the rarity, with drought being thought of as the norm. Gardeners that live in those regions practice xeric gardening methods in preparation for drought that is sure to come.

In areas that are typically rainfall-rich, the gardener and the plants are not prepared for the many problems that arise when less-than-average precipitation occurs. Plants that live there, accustomed to getting all the water they need, send out new soft, lush growth quickly. A break in the regular watering pattern causes an immediate reaction. Wilt occurs quickly, ramped up by loss of water through evaporation caused by increased air and soil temperatures. Most plants regain turgidity with a slow, deep drink of water. However, the cycle of wilt, stress, and watering takes its toll. Root systems stop producing deep-reaching roots, new roots collapse, eventually a plant's vascular system declines, leading to leaf drop, and the plant is not able to regain its foothold. Gardeners can only treat the symptoms when short droughts occur. The solution lies in planning for droughts long before they happen.

Top, left: **A horrific image of the devastation of the Dust Bowl Era.**
Top, right: **Reoccurring droughts in agricultural belts are common, threatening food and grain crops nationwide.**
Bottom: **Lake Mead, Nevada, provides water to over 20 million people living in Nevada and southern California. The drop in water level is evident by the exposed white stripe on the shoreline, which was under water just years before this photo was taken.**

## DWINDLING WATER RESOURCES

I have a gardening friend and professional affiliate in Southern California who told me, "Before I die, I want to live in a place where I don't have to continually be worried about drought and be plagued with water issues!" She better hurry to find that place, because we are running out of options.

Increased population, agriculture, damming, water diversion, pollution, saltwater intrusion, and overuse threaten our water supplies nationwide. The central portion of the U.S., which uses water supplied by the Ogallala Aquifer, has been experiencing low water tables and an accumulation of sediments. The Colorado and Rio Grande Rivers, major waterways for the Southwest and West Coast, no longer flow to the sea much of the year because water is diverted to support increased use. Reduced rainfall and snow deficits contribute to lowered water levels in reservoirs and lakes. Saltwater intrusion, affected by storm surges and increased population demands and withdrawals, has brought forth serious water quality issues in coastal aquifers that supply the East Coast states with potable water.

In a feature story aired by CBS's *60 Minutes* on November 16, 2014, titled "Depleting the Water," the threat of groundwater depletion was brought to light. Currently in the middle of one of the worst droughts in recorded history, California farmers have to dig two to three times deeper than before to find underground aquifers to support their wells. (When you dig a well, you are essentially drilling until you reach an aquifer, the underground water reservoir.) Farmers tap into shallow aquifers, which can be recharged after one season of average rainfall. But with droughts, they have had to dig to deeper aquifers, which take tens or hundreds of years to recharge.

No matter where you live, water budgets are stretched to the limit, and the price of gardening has gone up because of water. Long- and short-term drought, strained water resources, crumbling infrastructures, construction of new pipeline systems to move water, and supplying water to growing populations all contribute to water restrictions, lower water availability, and an increase in water costs.

## STRAINED WATER BUDGETS

According to WaterSense, an Environmental Protection Agency (EPA) Partnership Program, the majority of U.S. freshwater withdrawals are going to support thermo-electric power (41 percent), with irrigation of agricultural crops running a close second (37 percent), and domestic water use at 8.5 percent of the total. The average family uses over 300 gallons of water each day, *with roughly one-third of that going to water the landscape*. Water used outdoors to water our gardens fluctuates to account for periods of rainfall or drought.

# My Water-Smart Story

When my husband and I moved from California to southern Utah, we became acquainted with the system of water shares. Imagine our delight when our monthly water bills remained at a ridiculously low amount of $25 per month, only increasing to just under $100 during the triple-digit summer months. It seemed like someone had made a billing mistake. How could a place that was even more desert-like than southern California, that receives on average just 9 inches of rain each year, afford to supply water at those rates? We knew this living in the lap of water luxury would change.

Our log home is situated in the middle of a sloping 1½ acres, once covered in native sagebrush, juniper, and pine. Over the course of seven years, we designed and installed an irrigation and drainage system; built terraces, berms, and basins; carved out a vineyard, orchard, and kitchen, herb, and flower gardens; and blended native and low-water-use plants to form landscaped areas. It was (and is) an ongoing process to meet our goals of having food on the table, shade in the desert, and a green space that will be self-sustaining upon maturity. We both had education and experience that taught us how to garden on a water-conserving budget; the professional experiences that developed the skills needed to design, grow, and build water-thrifty landscapes; and we had *years* of hands-on experience gardening in a water-challenged arid climate. With those tools in hand, we began our journey.

Our small town, upon incorporation, began putting the wheels in motion to purchase two of three water companies that supplied our rural community. For a year before the purchase, monthly notices went out with estimates of how much we might expect to pay for water. It looked reasonable, we thought. Our first bill came in July for June water use. From $80 a month for the high-use month, which is when the vineyard, orchard, and vegetable gardens were growing full tilt, the bill was now $325! We were not prepared—not at all.

## GARDENING WITHIN OUR WATER BUDGET

When faced with this drastic increase in water costs, our immediate reaction was to jump into crisis water-management mode. The key to our quest to reduce our water consumption and water expense was to make the most of our water resources.

We turned off the irrigation timers on the landscape plantings. Fortunately, the trees, shrubs, and perennial beds were mature and well established. They barely skipped a beat in their growth or health and now live on supplemental watering only if they're showing signs of stress. This action alone cut the amount of landscape water use in half. The vegetable gardens require regular deep watering, so they remained on the irrigation timer with run times reduced, from 15 minutes twice daily to a bare minimum of 15 minutes watering in early morning hours. We monitored the plants for stress during the really hot days when supplemental watering was applied. Fortunately, July and August brought some monsoonal action, so for a few days out of each week, we were able to turn off the system in the vegetable garden completely. When we received our July/August bill, our water bill had been cut overall by 75 percent.

Here are the basics that helped us reach our goal of gardening within our water budget.

All of our landscapes and gardens are watered by drip or micro-spray systems that direct the water *slowly* and *directly* to the roots where it is needed. Overhead low-volume spray systems are used for turf and meadow areas.

The plants are watered deeply and regularly when they're immature to encourage deep-reaching root systems, which will allow the mature plants to survive on natural rainfall. Mature plantings receive supplemental watering on an as-needed basis.

Exposed soil surfaces are covered with mulch. Depending upon the plant type, weed barrier cloth, gravel, stone, leaves, tree trimmings, straw, and chipped or shredded bark cover the landscape and garden beds, orchard, vineyard, and pathways to minimize water loss and protect the soil from erosion and wind.

All plants are selected for their drought-tolerance. We looked for plants that live naturally in dry, arid, low rainfall climates, that have the structural advantages of deep root systems,

Top: **Planted ten years ago on a berm, this redbud tree is mature, strong, and healthy. It survives and thrives on natural rainfall (less than 10 inches a year), with supplemental watering only when there is a lack of monsoonal rains in the heat of summer.**

Bottom: **Planning for drought begins as the first plant goes into the ground.** Seasons of bringing the landscape to maturity and good health lead to a drought-tolerant, thriving garden in the future.

and have water-conserving characteristics such as coated or waxy leaves, serrated or deeply lobed leaf edges, or that produce oils—all characteristics of water-thrifty plants. (See Chapter 8, Water-Thrifty Plants).

We practice companion planting in the vegetable garden beds, interplant edibles in the landscape, and group plants in the landscape with similar water needs (zoning) to share resources.

We create shade and plant in the shady understories of trees, utilizing these moisture-saving microclimates.

We build and maintain drainage swales, berms and basins, and terraces in the landscape to minimize water runoff and to direct the flow of water.

We capture and use rainwater and snowmelt. A 50-gallon rain barrel fills in minutes with water running off the roof and can be used for supplemental hand-watering of landscape bed and container gardens. Snowmelt can be used for houseplants and greenhouse watering in winter.

# What Can *You* Do?

When faced with a gardening challenge, implement the "Straight As." Just having a plan to find a solution can bring a sigh of relief. If you are facing a long- or short-term drought, gardening in water-stressed areas that might be facing water rationing, or experiencing raising water costs, taking a few steps back to look at the garden objectively will go a long way toward finding helpful proactive solutions.

### ASSESS

Assess your current landscape. Conduct a garden inventory. Note the age, maturity, and health of trees, shrubs, and perennials, as they are the longest living plants in a garden. Look for overcrowding in beds or at plants that require constant pruning to limit their growth. Note open areas prone to weed invasion, water runoff, and erosion. Look for problem soils that tend toward dryness (sandy or grainy soils drain quickly) or are slow draining (you'll know that because a hole filled with water takes hours to drain). Look for unused spaces under eaves and trees that may provide microclimates or areas for interplanting edibles or other low-water use plantings.

### AUDIT

Applying water deeply and directing its flow is key to establishing a garden that can withstand drought and water deficits. If you have a functioning irrigation system, seek a professional to perform a water audit. Water authorities, conservation districts, water suppliers, university Extension agents, and public agencies often offer trained auditors who'll visit your home free of charge. An irrigation system audit will determine the efficiency of your system, if the water is distributed evenly, and if the water pressure is adequate to activate the system. Auditors may also make recommendations as to irrigation system design, repair, maintenance, and scheduling.

### ADJUST

Adjusting sprinkler heads, repairing broken or cracked PVC pipe, replacing valve diaphragms, removing worn-out pressure regulators, cleaning filters, and replacing emitters or worn drip

Left: The typical landscape of days gone by includes an expanse of lawn, thirsty shrubs and trees, and a concrete driveway that allows the water to run freely to the street.

Right: These drought-tolerant boxwood shrubs were quite small when planted from one-gallon containers, so the space was taken up with mulch and annual plantings as they grew into their natural form and mature size. As the water-smart garden matures, maintenance chores lessen.

lines are chores that take little time and effort. These problems drastically affect the efficiency of irrigation systems. Spray systems should be checked while they are running to adjust and redirect the spray or to unclog a nozzle. Drip system failures are more difficult to detect, as they are often covered with soil or mulch. If an emitter forces its way out of tubing, it may make itself visible with washed-out soil at the puncture or by wilting plants downstream on the system that are not receiving water. Check the systems weekly for clogs, breaks, and gushing or spurting water. Check plants for signs of wilt. Weekly monitoring and adjustments will save water, money, and your plants.

## ADAPT

Most plants in a garden get more water than they really need, but this doesn't mean you should cut them off entirely when water supplies are scarce. Even the most drought-tolerant plants need water to live. The trick is to give them *only* as much water as they need to survive and to apply it where and when they need it. Check the soil with your index finger for moisture—is the soil dry? If so, then water slowly and deeply. Plants have defense mechanisms that help them adapt to drought stress. Some go into dormancy by dropping their leaves, as is the case with native plants that are dormant during the summer. Some drought-tolerant plants slow their growth and stop generating new foliage. Others may lose their deep green color, fading to gray-green and becoming semi-dormant, as do lawns.

Routine gardening tasks need to be adapted to minimize plant stress during periods of less water. Let the lawn grow tall so the blades provide shade to the roots. Put away the pruners and allow the plants to grow into their natural form. Allow leaf litter to remain under trees—it is nature's mulch. Sweep the walkways instead of washing them. Repot rootbound plants in containers so they need less water, and move them to the shade. Don't fertilize during periods of drought; you want to discourage rapid new growth that requires more water to grow. Adapt to the drought-tolerant garden by minimizing your garden tasks, allowing the plants to grow naturally.

# Designing Landscapes for Today & Planning for the Future

Early in my horticulture career, it seemed as though southern California was the tropical paradise of a landscaper's dreams. We planted every square inch of ground with some sort of greenery, be it large, boisterous shrubs; expanses of "so green it hurts your eyes" turf; or borders jammed with flat after flat of colorful annuals. Landscape maintenance entailed hours each week of cutting back miles of ivy groundcover, its rampant growth encouraged by huge amounts of water applied by impact sprinklers running full tilt on a daily basis. The landscape industry thrived, nurseries couldn't stock enough plants, and pallet after pallet of Kentucky bluegrass went out the sod farm gates.

Then came the late 1980s and a seven-year drought. Lawns were pulled out and concrete and gravel poured in. Landscape designers planned hardscapes—no irrigation required. Nurseries struggled to survive on a cactus and succulent inventory, but a great many closed their doors. Sod farms were quiet, trying to find a way to win favor back into homeowners' hearts. Landscapers struggled, not knowing how to market their skills in a declining market.

The industry rallied, partnering with others who have experienced drought before. The principles of xeriscape and low-water-use landscapes were introduced and put into practice. Programs were developed at colleges and universities to educate the professionals and the public on the virtues of making the most out of the water they have, while encouraging them to grow green spaces for the future.

Twenty years later, fast forward to a thriving nursery industry that offers drought-tolerant, hardy, and less demanding plant materials. The result was cutting-edge irrigation principles and practices; water-thrifty and environmentally sound landscapes; and the continued quest by educational and research facilities to investigate new plants, materials, and theories devoted to conserving water and to creating sustainable green environments.

Those gardens of yesteryear have a new face. The design has been altered to include permeable hardscapes, textural interest of varied mulches, and a diverse color palette that spans all shades of greens, grays, golden amber, and crisp white. Open beds feature the perfect silhouette of a strongly branched tree, drifts of swaying ornamental grasses, and masses of blooming drought-, wind-, and heat-tough shrubs. Clusters of perennials and annuals that serve as pollinator magnets are blended with edibles to share resources.

Today's gardens are so much more than just shades of green filling a space. They are tough, healthy, sustaining landscapes, more diverse than ever, with seasonal interest at all times of the year. It is an exciting, challenging time for a gardener and for our gardens, making the planning an equally gratifying journey.

---

**A water-wise landscape is tough, durable, self-sustaining, beautiful, and lush.**

Water-smart landscaping techniques are enhanced by water-thrifty plants that fit beautifully with any garden style.

# CHAPTER 2

# Inspiration Gallery

## WATER-SMART LANDSCAPES
## FOR EVERY GARDEN STYLE

a VISION OF A LANDSCAPE style might be a sea of gravel surrounding stately prickly cactus or palm trees swaying in the breeze, creating an undulating pattern of color. Or maybe it is a shady retreat with a natural wood-beamed structure covered in grapevines. Your landscape style can be all you envision it to be, while being water-smart too.

As you peruse this gallery, consider what is behind the scenes of the finished landscape style and how all the pieces fall together—beautifully and water efficiently. Contouring the land with swales, berms, and basins directs the flow of water, adding depth, definition, and contrast to the landscape. Preparation of the soil before planting increases drainage and water movement in the soil, contributing to the health of the plants. Drip-irrigation systems direct the water to the roots where the plants need it. Mulched beds provide a finished look to the landscape, while cooling the soil and minimizing water loss. Permeable garden paths allow the water to be absorbed into the soil, while diminishing and filtering storm water runoff. Microclimates, created by overhead structures or by shade from a strongly branched tree, offer cool sitting spaces while providing homes for shade- and higher-moisture-loving plants. And finally, plants that define the style also have drought-tolerant characteristics that make them water thrifty.

Pictured here are healthy, thriving, mature landscapes. They are planned spaces, designed with the goal of having a lush, beautiful garden that will one day support itself on the water nature provides. Start patiently with small plants, giving them the seasons they need to grow deep and far-reaching root systems. Or go for immediate gratification and plant large specimens, providing the plants with a deep, well-draining soil to ease their establishment in the garden until they can stand on their own. Start with a look, a style you desire, and a budget you can afford, and build from there. Designing a water-smart garden in your style is a journey. Embrace it!

# Garden Style: *Mediterranean*

From the coastal regions of the Mediterranean Sea, this garden style gets its inspiration from the plants that grow naturally in temperate climates of Italy, France, Greece, Spain, southern Africa, and the islands of Sicily, Corsica, Cypress, and Crete. The Mediterranean style reflects easy, casual living with natural, flowing walkways, cooling shady arbors that protect from the sun, outdoor garden rooms for lounging and dining, and the soothing sound of a garden fountain. Mediterranean-style landscapes are lived-in gardens where most of life takes place outdoors.

Colors range from lavender and all shades of purple, bright yellow, pink, magenta, crisp white, gray-green, and silver-green with complimentary earth tones in gray, burnt orange, rich brown, to tan, olive green, with bold accents in cobalt blue, deep maroon, and white. The garden beds are finished with mulches in river rock, gravel, chipped or shredded bark, and decomposed granite. Dramatic hardscape materials give the design structure with terracotta pavers, rock walls, brightly painted stucco, colorful tiles, concrete pillars, natural stone walkways, beamed arbors with notched details, fire rings, fireplaces, and fountains.

# Garden Style: *Desert Xeric*

Desert xeric gardens utilize brilliant sunrises and sunsets to illuminate stately cactus and prickly desert trees. Boulders dot the scape, with undulating hills and arroyos forming natural dry stream beds lined with open-branched shrubs and swaying grasses. Spring brings masses of blooms that cover the desert scape, and shady arbors, courtyards, and patios create cool respites from the summer sun.

Colors are bold in vibrant yellow, red, deep purple, blue, and orange. Plant foliage is gray-green to white, with finely cut, lobed, and feathery leaves to soften edges. Cactus and strongly structured desert trees bring drama to the landscape. Mulches and pathways are natural decomposed granite, sand, and river rock. Boulders are used either singly as focal points or grouped for natural outcroppings to shape a dry stream bed. Varying colored river rock, cobalt blue or brilliant green glass pebbles, terracotta, and crushed cinder rock brings movement to the stream bed. Benches of wood, concrete, stone, and tiles take advantage of the shade from nearby evergreen trees, arbors, and overhead structures. Small fountains in courtyards create cool and calming oases, with cozy fire rings and fireplaces situated in open areas to let in the desert stars.

# Garden Style: *Southwestern*

Southwestern landscape style combines natural rugged elements reflective of the changing terrain and climate of the southwest. Outdoor spaces are made for comfort at all times of the year, with fireplaces to warm the hands; garden walls to bring shelter from wind; and shady, covered patios to provide a cool respite from the summer sun. Plantings blend drought-, heat-, and wind-tolerant native plants: conifers from colder climes in the high mountain regions, season-long blooming perennials, deciduous plants that offer brilliant fall foliage, and trees and shrubs with strong branching structures to provide winter interest.

Natural stones and boulders provide building materials for walls, raised beds, benches, dry stream beds, waterfalls, and ponds. Green walls enclose a space, and overhead vines make shaded seating areas. Colors, reflective of nature's landscape, are terracotta to brick red, varying shades of deep to pale green, sunny to golden yellow, brilliant to burnt orange, gray to silvery white, and soft beige to brown. A blending of western and Native American influences provides colorful and bold accents. Mulches finish the beds in shredded bark, river and cinder rock, sand, and gravel. Garden paths are natural, compacted terracotta-colored soil, pavers, decomposed granite, and stone.

# Garden Style: *Cottage*

Cottage-style landscapes are full of color and movement. Curving pathways separate expanses of free-flowing blooming or foliage plants that are interplanted in drifts or grouped in masses without defined boundaries. Also called an English cutting garden, the abundance of blooms makes this landscape beg to be brought indoors in large bouquets. Cottage-style landscapes are designed so each plant is defined, while merging naturally and beautifully with its neighbor. Color adds emphasis with swaths of brightly colored blooms drifting from one to another, or blended together in a rich tapestry of color that fills the space.

Cottage gardens are a riot of color, with soft shades of lavender, pink, yellow, cream, and peach blended together or combined with richer hues. Small trees provide focal points and a bit of dappled shade for flowering plants that need it, and large shrubs make green walls to enclose the area. White picket fences, ironwork railings, willow arbors, and grapevine trellises provide accents rather than boundaries, with plants tumbling over, leaning against, or climbing upon their forms. Mulch and pathways are gravel, stone, or decomposed granite. Whimsical and eclectic colorful garden art draws the eye to garden vignettes.

# Garden Style: *Formal/Modern*

A formal/modern garden style makes a bold statement with an emphasis on geometric forms, order, and structure. Linear, soft, turf-covered garden paths run adjacent to blocks of garden beds that are defined by sheared, green hedges. Groupings of singular species are closely planted together into symmetrical shapes. Color is achieved through differences in leaf color, as well as in varying textures and shapes. There are few flowering plants needed in this design statement, but they do have a place here, enclosed by green garden walls that bring the varying bloom colors together in a controlled and defined space.

Clear, crisp white is a must-have to make the green pop in this garden. Tall, stately clipped hedges, topiary shrubs, and pollarded trees with strong structural details enclose garden rooms to house benches in iron or wood, provide focal points, or to line a path. White gravel and stone mulches add to the garden formality. Quiet reflecting pools, the gentle trickle of a fountain, and soft landscape lighting give the formal garden a new face for night viewing. Statues, cement, marble, and granite pillars and urns, iron scrollwork, arbors, and rails provide accents in an organized, soothing, and quiet space.

# Garden Style: *Prairie*

The prairie garden style is open to the sky and nature's landscape, allowing access to wind, sun, and stars. Drifts of annuals and perennials, interplanted with ornamental grasses, shrubs that rustle in the breeze, and trees with open branch habits create a flowing, moving landscape that transitions seamlessly into its surroundings. Prairie gardens are xeric gardens that shine throughout the seasons. Large open spaces provide room for the prairie garden to establish itself, but a prairie can also be reproduced as meadow plantings in smaller spaces.

Plant colors of all hues and shades are enhanced by grouping species together in stands, just as plants colonize in nature. Flowering plants provide spring and summer blooms. Tall, clumping grasses remain in autumn gold shades throughout the winter for seasonal interest. Natural split rail fencing, willow arbors, and benches are functional as well as artistic elements. Gravel, stone, and chipped or shredded bark are used as bed mulch, to line garden paths, and to provide surface for sitting, dining, and star-watching. Natural boulders bring contour to the otherwise flat to gently undulating terrain. Long, open wood porches and decks are perfect for lounging and garden viewing.

# Garden Style: *Woodland*

Woodland garden style mimics nature in soft, pine needle-lined pathways meandering through forested, shady groves. From dappled sun to full shade to small sunny openings, woodland gardens are cool spaces for quiet sitting and for wandering aimlessly down garden paths. Low, lush borders of foliage plants intermingled with flowering groundcovers and forest bulbs cover the woodland floor. Vines run rampant, climbing over trellises and fences and tumbling into paths. Shrubs form dense stands in the understories of tall trees, where a trickling stream dotted with lichen-covered stones ebbs and flows. The woodland garden is a serene and cool space, at home with nature that has run amok.

Woodland gardens include all shades and hues of green, with white and silver accents, pops of bright red, orange, and purple, and drifts of soft lavender, pale pink, and ivory. Cool and soft colors are understated and are often hidden among dense foliage. Mulch is provided by nature in pine needles, shredded bark, pine cones, twigs, and leaves. Logs, twisted branches, and lichen-covered boulders provide garden art. Benches are of log or rough wood and are scattered along the pathway edge or sited under the seclusion of a vine-covered arbor.

This terrace garden, a residence in San Diego, California, directs the flow of water, supplied by drip irrigation, to the drought-tolerant plantings, minimizing runoff and providing structural integrity to the steep slope.

# CHAPTER 3

# Water-Smart Design Solutions

aLL PLANTS NEED WATER to survive. To make the most out of water resources, though, we cannot allow it to have its way while it flows freely down the gutters, fills driveways and patios, or takes the soil with it as it runs in rivulets through the garden. The solution is to *direct the flow*. We want to make sure we are directing the water to where it is needed and that we keep it there until the plants use it.

I remember my first sight of the desert as my family migrated from the Pacific Northwest to Arizona. What I envisioned about living in a desert was what I had seen in movies: a vast wasteland of sand with the occasional prickly cactus standing tall in the shimmering heat. Imagine my surprise to learn we had been traveling in the desert for over 100 miles before I realized that we were in one.

There were clumps of low-lying cactus growing in colonies, nestled in basins formed by undulating hills of sand. Sweeps of gray- to white-stemmed bushes grew on sandy berms, with deep roots anchoring them in. Rock outcroppings, edged by swaying grasses and burned by the sun and wind to varying colors of amber, brown, and burgundy, provided texture and drama. There were groups of Joshua trees standing tall, their "arms" reaching to the sky, while the desert floor was blanketed in tiny yellow blooms. Swales with rocks and pebbles dotting their sides formed shallow dry streambeds that seemed to flow through the desert. It was not *at all* the barren desert scene I'd imagined!

Where desert plants grow naturally gives clues as to how they survive on little water. Nature-made berms provide volumes of soft sand to send out long roots to the moisture that lies deep within the soil profile. These roots anchor the plants, holding them firm in strong desert winds. The basins that form naturally beneath the berms capture moisture as it runs off the

Left: **Machu Picchu illustrates the ancient practice of terrace gardening to support life.**
Right: **A desert trail at Desert Springs Preserve in Las Vegas, Nevada, full of green and lush plants; not at all the wasteland I imagined a desert to be.**

dry earth during spring rains, encouraging plants that require more water to nest there. Rock outcroppings shade and cool the soil beneath, slowing the rate of evaporation and holding just enough moisture for shallow-rooting grasses to grow en masse. Berms, swales, and catch basins that mimic nature's design can provide the same benefits in the garden, to direct, slow, and capture the water's flow.

Harvesting, storing, and using rainwater is just one method Native Americans used to bring water to their crops in arid environments. Rainwater catchment systems, dug out of the earth and carved from rocks, called "waffle gardens," housed thirstier edible crops. "Trincheras" were terraces built along mountainsides to capture runoff and on riverbanks to take advantage of overflow during flooding.

The terraced farms on the mountainside in Machu Picchu illustrate this ancient practice, dating as far back as 1,500 years. Terrace gardening, the ultimate example of sustainable gardening on steep slopes, controls erosion and minimizes water runoff by directing the flow of water to each "terrace" as the water moves. The materials used to form the shallow retaining walls also absorb heat from the sun, forming a microclimate that diminishes the effects of frost. This age-old, ingenious gardening technique can be easily translated into our home landscape.

With water supplies either diminished, threatened, or taxed by drought, it just makes good sense to utilize rainwater as much as we can. Lessons learned from nature's desert plants, borrowed ideas from ancient civilizations, adapted methods learned from pioneers, and new technological advances all help conserve by directing the flow of water.

# Direct the Flow: Berms and Catch Basins

Berms provide water-saving benefits by slowing and directing the flow of water: they form a barricade that stops the water from flowing freely across the soil surface, taking the soil with it. The redirected water flows into an adjoining catch basin, where it is held until it can percolate down into the soil profile. Berms and catch basins direct the flow of water, reducing soil erosion and making it available to the roots of plants where they need it. Catch basins can be earthworks or manufactured, such as those used in drainage systems to capture the directed water. (See the section Drainage Systems, Permeable Surfaces, page 50.)

## BERMS AND CATCH BASINS
## FOR TREES AND SHRUBS

When you plant a tree or shrub, it is a common practice to surround it with berm, forming a basin to hold water. Without this system in place, when we water the plant, the water flows across the surface of the soil and *away* from the plant's roots, which is where the water needs to be. Capturing the water in a basin allows time for the soil to absorb the water and directs the flow downward so that it penetrates deeply into the soil. Simple in design, but very effective in directing the flow and capturing the water, berms and basins create healthier, stronger plants, protecting your investment and nurturing the landscape to be a water-smart garden in the future. (For detailed planting tips, see Chapter 7, Maintaining Water-Smart Gardens.)

## HOW TO BUILD A BERM AND BASIN
## FOR TREES AND SHRUBS

Anyone can build a berm and basin with just a shovel and some soil. After planting the plant at exactly the same level it was when in the container, build a berm using the native soil. The berm goes completely around the drip line of the plant (the farthest point to where the branches extend), providing the support "walls" that form a catch basin that "catches" and holds the water. A berm should be 4 to 8 inches tall when it's finished.

Tree roots extend far beyond the drip line as they mature, but just after planting, the root zone is confined to a smaller area, and that is where you want to catch and direct the water. The circumference of the berm should be made larger as a tree or shrub matures to allow water to percolate throughout the entire soil mass surrounding the rootball. For example, the berm for our dwarf peach tree at planting time measured 3 feet across to accommodate its bare-root mass of 6 inches. After three years, it was 6 feet across, and at its mature size eight years later, the berm measures roughly 12 feet across.

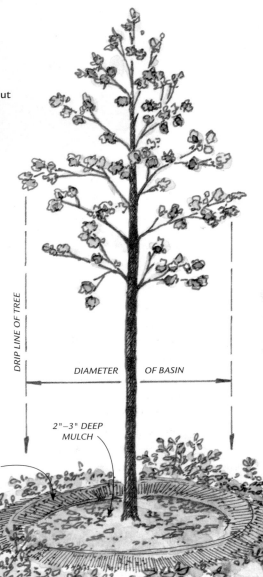

The berm is made of existing soil and extends beyond the tree drip line, forming a broad basin around the tree to hold water. The basin is topped with mulch to maintain soil moisture, to cool the soil and roots, and to minimize loss of water by evaporation.

## BERMS AND CATCH BASINS IN THE LANDSCAPE

Berms in the landscape are longer, taller, and wider than those of the tree and shrub berms, and the catch basins are deeper and broader. The goal is the same—to collect and store water. Berms can be used when building landscape beds. Surrounding the bed with a berm

Top: **The berm in the background forms the walls of the basin. A rain garden survives on water runoff from the berm and from rainwater captured in the basin.**
Bottom: **The berm was built over a three-year period from twigs, green debris, and soil, creating a well-drained, deep soil for drought-tolerant plantings and forming a broad basin for the meadow.**

contains the water, and the resulting basin becomes the planting space. Rain gardens have become a design feature in many drought-tolerant landscapes as a way to capture rainwater and use it for plantings. A deep catch basin is dug first, and the excavated soil is used to build the berm. The berm and basin are home to plants that use the rainwater as their sole source of water.

Larger berms are earthworks that support trees, shrubs, and landscape plants. In areas with problem soils, berms are built using imported soil, creating a deep base of well-draining soil that can support deep-rooting plants. The berms help create a drought-tolerant, healthy landscape that might otherwise be riddled with ongoing problems of poorly draining, nutrient-deficient, or saline soils. The underlying goal of creating a water-smart landscape is creating healthy environments in which the plants can grow. Berms and basins are one solution to achieving the goal.

This landscape berm is built short, approximately 8 to 12 inches tall, surrounding a broad, shallow basin 20 to 30 feet in diameter that captures and holds rainwater. The water slowly percolates into the soil, supporting the plants growing in the basin.

## HOW TO BUILD A BERM AND CATCH BASIN IN THE LANDSCAPE

Constructing a berm depends upon your energy level, materials available, and your pocketbook! To build a landscape berm and basin, you need the space to accommodate the supporting dimensions, soil, and a shovel, hoe, and rake. Larger berms can be created by hand over a long period by mounding up green waste and soil, compacting, and adding water to speed up the decomposition and settling. If you lack the time for a berm-in-progress, you can rent the equipment and do the work in one day's time. You can also hire a contractor to bring in the necessary soil or excavate it from your property and move it to the site. The contractor will provide compaction and rough grade with its equipment, and you can save some money by doing the final grade with your rake. If designing the berm and basin is a daunting task, hire a landscape designer to design the plan to scale with construction details; then you can build it yourself.

Materials for building berms can be soil of any type *except* sand, which would not hold its shape over a long period. If you are excavating or landscaping, use the soil you remove from projects to build the berm. If you are plagued with large amounts of clay or waterlogged, lean, or poorly structured soils, then importing clean fill soil may be necessary to build the berm.

Building landscape berms requires some planning and measuring, plus a plan drawn to scale. Use a garden hose to outline the berm and provide a good visual of its shape and size. Berms that are too small end up looking like little anthill mounds, out of proportion and not accomplishing their function. Scale and slope are critical to minimize water runoff and erosion. The higher the berm, the wider and broader the base needs to be. The rule of thumb is that a berm 6 inches tall needs to be at least 24 inches wide at its base. In easy math: for every inch or foot of height, you need four times that measurement for the base. This calculation also ensures that the berm will not have overly steep sides, which makes them subject to caving in or eroding away with the first good rain. The height of a larger earthworks berm should not exceed 4 feet after compaction with a width of the base at 16 feet. Taller mounds of soil require retaining walls to hold their shape and to control erosion.

1 Choose a site, size, and shape for the rain garden, following the design standards outlined on the previous two pages. Use rope or a hose to outline the rain garden excavation area. Avoid trees and be sure to stay at least 10 ft. away from permanent structures. Try to choose one of the recommended shapes: crescent, kidney, or tear drop.

2 Dig around the perimeter of the rain garden and then excavate the central area to a depth of 4 to 8 in. Heap excavated soil around the garden edges to create a berm on the three sides that are not at the entry point. This allows the rain garden to hold water during a storm.

3 Dig and fill sections of the rain garden that are lower, working to create a level foundation. Tamp the top of the berm so it will stand up to water flow. The berm eventually can be planted with grasses or covered with mulch.

4 Level the center of the rain garden and check with a long board with a carpenter's level on top. Fill in low areas with soil and dig out high areas. Move the board to different places to check the entire garden for level. Note: If the terrain demands, a slope of up to 12% is okay. Then, rake the soil smooth.

5 Plant specimens that are native to your region and have a well-established root system. Contact a local university extension or nursery to learn which plants can survive in a saturated environment (inside the rain garden). Group together bunches of 3 to 7 plants of like variety for visual impact. Mix plants of different heights, shapes, and textures to give the garden dimension. Mix sedges, rushes, and native grasses with flowering perennials. The plants and soil cleanse stormwater that runs into the garden, leaving pure water to soak slowly back into the earth.

6 Apply double-shredded mulch over the bed, avoiding crowns of new transplants. Mulching is not necessary after the second growing season. Complement the design with natural stone, a garden bench with a path leading to it, or an ornamental fence or garden wall. Water a newly established rain garden during drought times—as a general rule, plants need 1 in. of water per week. After plants are established, you should not have to water the garden. Maintenance requirements include minor weeding and cutting back dead or unruly plant material annually.

WATER-SMART DESIGN SOLUTIONS

WATER FLOW

This diversion swale follows the path of water. A shallow depression allows the water to percolate, diverting and slowing the flow of water while forming a natural-looking dry stream bed.

## DIVERSION SWALES

A diversion swale is similar to a berm and basin. Instead of storing the water until it is absorbed, like a basin, the water moves down the swale, where it is redistributed (diverted) to a designated spot, such as a planter bed, garden, or lawn. Diversion swales serve two functions:

1. They divert and slow the flow of water as it moves down slopes and hills.
2. They capture water in a swale that allows it to percolate into the soil.

Diversion swales that direct runoff water can be a design feature in the landscape. Landscaped with boulders and stones, lined with sand (like a real streambed) and river rock, and planted with ornamental grasses and other drought-tolerant plantings, a swale becomes a meandering, beautiful, dry streambed. Use a swale as a pathway in the landscape: add 4 inches of permeable material, then tamp or roll to provide firm footing. Swales can also be installed at the end of drainage pipes to divert the runoff to another source.

## HOW TO BUILD A DIVERSION SWALE

Diversion swales are made of existing soil and lined with gravel, stone, or other permeable materials that allow water to percolate into the soil. They are shallower and broader than a trench, which is more apt to house a drain line than it is to move water to another location.

Decide where you need the swale, and if it will be a part of the landscape or purely functional. Lay out the pattern using string or garden hose. All you need is a shovel, a hoe, a grading rake, and moist soil. If possible, build the diversion swale just after a good rain; any eroded area provides a template for the direction of the swale. Use the center of the eroded area as a starting point to dig a shallow trench—4 to 6 inches deep should be enough. Pull the soil away from the center and toward the edge, using a hoe if the ground is soft enough. Use the soil you scrape from the center for the sides.

The swale can be as wide as you want; just make sure the edges are mounded high enough to support the swale, yet not so high as to wash out or erode. After digging the swale, test it by running water slowly down it. If the water stops flowing and begins to puddle, dig the swale deeper to allow the water to gain momentum and pass freely. A good amount will percolate into the soil as it makes it way down the swale, but in a good rain, there will be some discharge at the end. Flowerbeds, tree basins, lawn areas, groundcover spaces, or herb or vegetable gardens are good discharge spots that could always use a bit of extra water. Fill the swale with gravel to meet the existing grade, raking it smooth to avoid tripping hazards.

## TERRACES

When the terrain is sloping and berms and basins can't do the job needed to control the flow of water down the hill, terraces provide a viable alternative. Terraces are broad steps, running along the contours of the slope. The terrace is cut into the slope, and the flat bench that remains becomes the planting space. The water spans out over the bench, percolating into the soil. Terraces are problem-solvers for homeowners who have slopes and hills for their planting spaces and for conserving the water used to irrigate steep inclines. Steep slopes that put a home under threat of landslides caused by unsettled soils or poor compaction can be corrected through the use of terracing and retaining wall systems.

Very steep slopes with a 2:1 ratio (for every 2 feet of horizontal travel, the slope drops 1 foot) would require the assistance of an engineer and the skills of a landscape contractor. Engineering is necessary to determine the cuts into the slope and to calculate the load-bearing limits of the walls. Retaining walls need to be built strong enough to support tons of soil and plant materials.

## HOW TO BUILD A TERRACE

For less steep inclines, homeowners can successfully design and build terraces. Terraces need a well-draining soil: if that isn't already present, amended soil should be added to ensure good drainage. Landscapes that have waterlogged or heavy clay soils may require imported soil to build the terrace, as both these soil types can lead to structural breakdown and slippage, contributing to landslides.

Short terraces, under 2 feet tall, may be built using stone, rock, or logs dry stacked to support the terrace. There are also numerous engineered retaining wall block systems that can take the weight and come with detailed instructions on building the wall. If you are using logs or lengths of lumber, secure each tier with rebar to anchor it for stability. Check your local building codes before you begin construction to make sure you are in compliance. You may

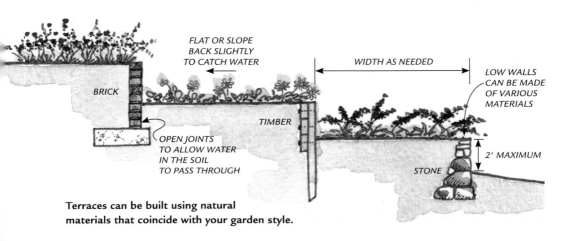

**Terraces can be built using natural materials that coincide with your garden style.**

This side view illustrates construction details. Permeable materials for retaining walls are spaced and dry stacked, without the use of concrete or mortar. With this method, water can flow freely into the soil.

decide that a shorter retaining wall will suffice and be easier for you to build yourself. If a taller wall is better suited to your needs, hire a designer and contractor so that it is in compliance.

Sketch out the area on paper to determine the approximate location of the terrace. If more than one terrace will be used, lay out the topmost terrace first. Using flags or string line, outline each terrace on the slope before beginning work. If you are able to use existing rocks or boulders as wall supports, then incorporate them into the terrace. If there is existing vegetation and the soil is stable, then terraces may be nothing more than short shallow steps, hand-carved into a slope, providing small pockets of planting spaces and requiring no additional wall supports.

The steeper the slope, the more shallow the cut will be. Dig the bottom terrace first, working your way up the slope. The first retaining wall is set directly on the ground, then the next terrace is dug above it, allowing you to pile the soil on the terrace below while you build each successive wall. Make sure the wall on the bottom of the slope is level. This will ensure that any successive walls and terraces will be level as well. Once the first retaining wall is laid, backfill and level out the soil on the terrace.

Tamp the soil tightly along the wall to ensure the soil will stay in place. Add a few inches of soil, moisten if it's dry, tamp it in, then repeat the process until the soil level is about 6 inches from the top of the wall. The extra 6 inches will be used for planting and mulch. If there will be another terrace above the first, then wait to do the final grading and backfilling until you have completed the next terrace. The bottom terrace is a good spot to pile the soil taken from the second terrace. After building the second terrace, use the piled soil to complete the backfill process on the first level, bringing the soil to the desired level.

# HOW TO BUILD A STONE TERRACE WALL

1 Dig into the slope to create a trench for the first wall. Reserve the soil you remove nearby—you'll want to backfill with it when the wall is done.

2 Level the bottom of the trench and measure to make sure you've excavated deeply enough.

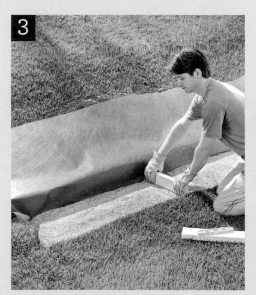

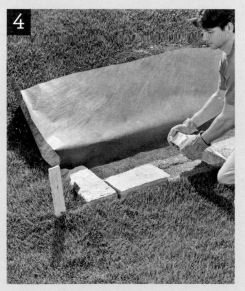

3 After compacting a base, cover the trench and hill slope with landscape fabric, and then pour and level a 1-in. layer of coarse sand.

4 Place the first course of stones in rough position. Run a level mason's string at the average height of the stones.

5 Add or remove gravel under each stone to bring the front edges level with the mason's string.

6 Begin the second course with a longer stone on each end so the vertical gaps between stones are staggered over the first course.

7 Finish out the second course. Use shards and chips of stone as shims where needed to stabilize the stones. Check to make sure the ½-in. setback is followed.

8 Finish setting the return stones in the second course, making adjustments as needed for the return to be level.

9 Backfill behind the wall with river rock or another good drainage rock.

10 Fold the landscape fabric over the drainage rock (the main job of the fabric is to keep soil from migrating into the drainage rock and out the wall) and backfill behind it with soil to level the ground.

11 Trim the landscape fabric just behind the back of the wall.

12 Finish the wall by capping it off with some of your nicer, long flat stones. Bond them with block-and-stone adhesive.

13 Level off the soil behind the wall with a garden rake. Add additional walls if you are terracing.

Left: **A catch basin allows water to flow through the slatted lid that slows the entrance of debris. The water is then captured in the small basin underground that further collects debris. Then the water passes through the outlet and into the attached drainpipe.**
Right: **A catch basin with a forged iron lid becomes artwork in the stone patio, while doing its job to direct the rainwater to the drainpipe below. The lid is pried up once a month to clean the debris collected in the catch basin.**

# Drainage Systems

Most residential construction is in strict compliance with county and city ordinances regarding water drainage and storm water runoff. Most homes are built on a pad, and the final grade ensures that water flows away from the structure. Storm water drainage systems fall under the responsibility of city municipalities. Any drainage systems built within the property line should not conflict or compromise the infrastructure drainage systems already in place. Before any drainage is installed within your property boundaries, visit the city or county offices to locate existing systems and for guidelines for installation of landscape drainage systems.

Underground drainage systems are another way of capturing the flow of water and moving it to another location. A common drainage system is to capture the water that comes out of the downspout, moving it through a drain pipe to another location where it can be put to use in the landscape. If there is a great amount of rainwater, then a manufactured catch basin (not to be confused with the earthworks catch basin previously discussed) is installed. The catch basin captures debris that may be in the water, allowing the water to pass through the discharge outlet and move on its way.

Hardscape features that puddle with water, poorly draining soils that turn mucky, grading malfunctions that lead to pooling water, sloped terrains with erosion problems, and excessive rainwater runoff may be diminished with an underground drainage system. In order to capture and control as much water as possible, using drainage systems that work in tandem with other earthworks methods makes the best use of water resources. If you are unsure about how to solve a drainage problem, hire an architect or contractor to design and install the best drainage system for your situation.

### OUR BASIC DRAINAGE SYSTEM

At my home, we have a short drainage pipe that runs down the side of a sloped wheelbarrow path that is also fed by water runoff passing through a drain located in a seating alcove. The pipe then continues under a paved patio, runs along the back of the house, feeds into a large drainpipe running under the house, and finally discharges into a drainage swale at the front of the house. Because there can be quite a lot of water moving through the pipe, we have also installed a couple of catch basins to filter out the accumulation of juniper berries and twigs. The only maintenance of the system is to clean out the basins periodically to allow the system to do its job.

## HOW TO BUILD A DRAINAGE SYSTEM

The first step is to determine where the water is coming from, then to decide where you want the water to go. Never direct the water off your property into the street or into a neighbors' landscape. Lay out the path where the pipe will be, from beginning to end, then contact the utility and water companies to make sure you are not conflicting with power or service lines.

System components are readily available and relatively inexpensive for the work that they do. Corrugated pipe is flexible and easy to snake down a not-so-straight trench and in irregular terrains, but due to the corrugation, the inside walls are more apt to become clogged with debris. For short runs, it works well and the sections can be snapped together, no glue required. Sewer and drain pipe is more rigid and has smooth interior walls, so are less apt to clog. Drain pipe needs to be glued together. Perforated pipe is flexible or rigid, and has holes or slits. It is useful for subsurface drainage or for short runs, capturing and directing the flow of water, while allowing some water to percolate back into the soil.

Dig a trench at least 6 inches wide and slope it down 1 to 2 inches for every length of pipe so the water can flow freely. The depth of the trench needs to be at least 10 inches, deep enough to cover the pipe with soil or gravel and to avoid having the pipe crack if it is walked upon. If you live in colder climes, USDA Cold Hardiness Zones 5 and below, there is the risk of water freezing in the pipe in winter. Digging below the frost line might be impractical, but spring thaw will release the water. If you have a particularly rocky or hard soil, then rent a trencher to do the work.

When you buy the pipe, the supplier will help you select fittings for converting to drain pipes, coupling pipe together, and for integrating catch basins into the system. Lay out all the adapter fittings, pipe, and couplings, in the order they will go, alongside the trench. Attach the adapters first, then start gluing and adding pipe, section by section. After the system is completely set, then do a trial run by running a bit of water into the inlet, making sure the water flows down the pipe and out the end. Then bury the pipe, using soil or gravel to fill in the trench.

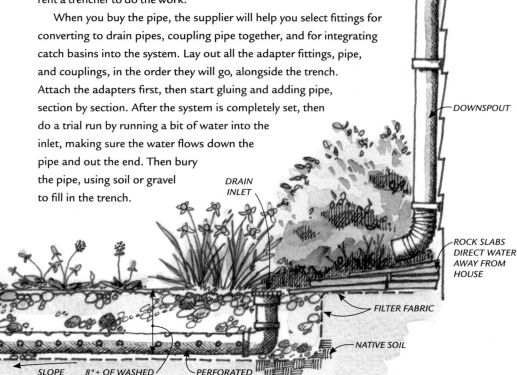

*DOWNSPOUT*

*DRAIN INLET*

*ROCK SLABS DIRECT WATER AWAY FROM HOUSE*

*FILTER FABRIC*

*NATIVE SOIL*

*SLOPE*  *8"+ OF WASHED GRAVEL*  *PERFORATED DRAIN PIPE*

**This drainage system directs the water coming from the home downspout away from the house into a length of perforated drainpipe that allows the water to percolate into the soil. The perforated pipe could be replaced with solid drain line, transporting the water to another destination in the landscape.**

Left: **A permeable path made of stone pavers, interplanted with** *Dymondia margaretae*. **Dymondia is a low-growing, ground-hugging perennial with a deep root system and gray-green leaves with white undersides, making it drought tolerant when established. It takes a bit of foot traffic. Hardier thyme would work in colder climes.**

Right: **A permeable pathway composed of white gravel allows water to be absorbed into the soil and provides architectural interest and contrast with the natural mulch beds.**

## PERMEABLE SURFACES

With concern about storm water runoff and water conservation in the landscape, permeable surfaces are fast becoming the preferred choice for hardscape features. Large expanses of driveway; sidewalks; and patio floors built with concrete, asphalt, and traditional brick, stone, or pavers set in concrete are subject to water runoff. As it flows off the surface, the water carries contaminates with it. Storm water runoff beyond your property line and into the street is within the domain of city municipalities, but there is much you can do to minimize water loss and storm water runoff in your landscape.

There are permeable surfaces to fit into every landscape style and situation. Instead of a concrete driveway, use permeable or porous concrete, made from concrete and water that forms a paste that surrounds aggregates. This creates more air pockets and spaces in the final, hardened product, allowing water to percolate into the soil. Interlocking pavers and plastic reinforced grids offer the strength of concrete, while allowing the water to penetrate the soil. Reinforced gridwork also has spaces for planting turf or other plants that can utilize the captured water.

Permeable bricks and pavers, along with permeable joint fillers, minimize water runoff and return the water to the soil, filtering it at the same time. Gravel, decomposed granite, stone, shredded bark, recycled wood, organic mulch, and sand are available in a wide range of textures and colors. These materials take the place of concrete and traditional paved and mortared patios and paths, slowing the flow of water off the surface and redirecting it down into the soil profile. Permeable pathways and surfaces include a layer of weed barrier cloth under the finished materials to deter weed growth and to provide a barrier between gravel, rock or other materials to stop them from infiltrating into the soil.

If you have expanses of concrete and you are retrofitting to a water-smart landscape, then use the broken pieces as pavers or to build retaining walls. Asphalt should be replaced with other permeable options, but have it hauled away to the appropriate landfill as it should not be re-used in the landscape. Build a path on an elevated berm; add a layer of permeable material that allows water to penetrate the soil and seep into the adjoining garden beds. Build a patio with traditional bricks, butting them up next to each other and use dry sand, broomed into the cracks (brick-on-sand), which allows the water to drain into the soil. Enhance a woodland scene by extending the mulched beds into a natural path lined with pine needles or shredded bark.

## HOW TO TO CREATE A PERMEABLE SURFACE

A permeable subbase looks a little like a typical compacted gravel subbase, but because the open-grade drainage rock is devoid of fines it does not form a solid layer and thus it allows water to run through, not off, it.

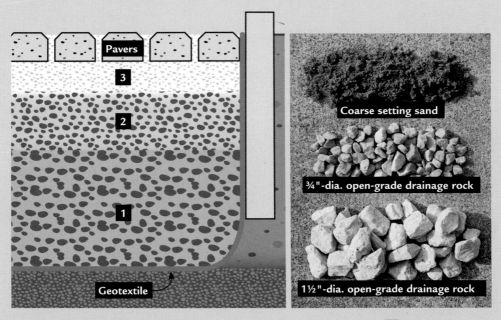

Left: **The components of a permeable subbase, from bottom to top, include 1 a 4- to 6-in. layer of 1½-in.-diameter, open-grade drainage rock (limestone is shown here); above that, 2 a 2- to 4-in. layer of open-grade rock; 3 a top layer of coarse sand or pulverized granite for use as a setting bed for flagstone or masonry units.**

Right: **The thickness of your permeable subbase depends on the soil conditions. For stable soil with good drainage, a 4- to 6-in. subbase is adequate. If you have loamy or sandy soil, go as thick as 10 in., with a layer of larger-diameter drainage rock. Adding an underlayment of geogrid textile will help stabilize the subbase in such cases. An underlayment is not helpful in stable soil with good drainage.**

**Line level**

**Minimum slope: ½-in. per 10 ft. away from house**

1 Drive corner posts and outline the patio area. Run mason's lines between the corner posts. Ideally, the patio should slope away from an adjoining house at a rate of around ½ in. for every 10 ft. Set a level line along the edges of the patio perpendicular to the house. Adjust the line downward to create the ¼ in. per 1-ft. slope.

**Story pole**

2 Begin excavating the site. A typical permeable subbase is 8 in. below grade when you allow for the thickness of the setting layer and the pavers or other surfacing. Use your layout strings to establish your digging depth. Measure the distance from the mason's line to the ground and add the depth of your excavation— 8 in. in the project seen here. Make a story pole with markings that match the distance from the planned bottom of the excavation to the mason's line. Keep the lines in place as you dig (this does create an obstacle but it is the best way to assure that you don't overdig).

3 Excavate the patio site using the story pole as a depth guide. Be sure to call (in the U.S., simply dial "811") and have any utility lines flagged before you begin digging. Be careful not to dig too deeply, as the best base for your subbase is undisturbed earth. Once the excavation is complete, remove the strings and prepare for the installation of the subbase.

4 A permeable base is made with open-grade rock, which is simply landscape rock that has no fines or binders, as typical subbase (often called Class V or Class II) does. The bottom layer should be rock that is not smooth and has diameters of 1½ to 2 in. Spread a 2- to 4-in.-deep layer of rock over the excavation area. OPTION: Install a layer of landscape fabric over the site to inhibit weeds. Landscape fabric can be installed under the subbase or on top of the subbase, but must be under the setting base layer.

5 Spread the rock out into an even layer. Use a garden rake or landscape rake to spread it. The subbase should extend past the planned edges of the project area by at least 10 in. on all open sides.

6 Tamp the rock to compact it. You can use a hand tamper, but for best results use a rented plate compactor. This is a very important part of creating a solid patio base, so be sure to be diligent with your efforts. Compact the rock as you go: do not compact more than 2 in. of material at one time. Wear foam ear plugs or other ear protection.

7 Add additional layers of large rock until the base layer is at least 4 in. thick. Then, switch to a smaller open-grade rock for the next layer. Here, ¾-in.-dia. buff limestone is being used. Add, spread, and compact the smaller-grade rock until the leveled surface follows the grade of the patio and the surface of the rock layer is 2 in., plus the thickness of your surfacing material, below grade at the top of the worksite. This completes your permeable subbase. Add a sand setting layer and pavers according to the demands of your project.

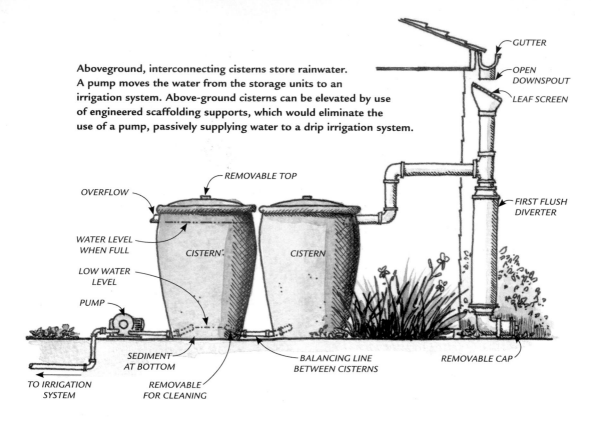

Aboveground, interconnecting cisterns store rainwater.
A pump moves the water from the storage units to an
irrigation system. Above-ground cisterns can be elevated by use
of engineered scaffolding supports, which would eliminate the
use of a pump, passively supplying water to a drip irrigation system.

GUTTER

OPEN
DOWNSPOUT

LEAF SCREEN

REMOVABLE TOP

OVERFLOW

FIRST FLUSH
DIVERTER

WATER LEVEL
WHEN FULL

CISTERN          CISTERN

LOW WATER
LEVEL

PUMP

SEDIMENT
AT BOTTOM

BALANCING LINE
BETWEEN CISTERNS

REMOVABLE CAP

TO IRRIGATION
SYSTEM

REMOVABLE
FOR CLEANING

# Harvest & Store Rainwater

Since the U.S. was formed, there have been laws prohibiting the capture and use of rainwater.
Each state had issues to solve, since it is their responsibility to regulate and govern water
use. There was confusion surrounding the laws, some having to do with water rights, others
concerned with the dangers of reusing rainwater. With water conservation being a concern
across the nation, every state has approved the capturing of rainwater off a homeowner's
roof. Colorado made harvesting rainwater legal in 2009. Utah legalized it in 2010, and
Washington state passed legislature approving it in 2011. Some states require online
registration if you are doing it; others don't have any permitting in place. Now, there are
programs being initiated across the nation offering rebate programs if homeowners capture,
store, and use rainwater. For specific state regulations and restrictions, be sure to contact
your state legislature.

The water that results from just ½-inch of rainfall falling on a 1,000-square-foot roof
amounts to over 280 gallons of water. Not only is that amount of water going to offset
water use in the landscape (by using non-potable water), it helps the environment as well by
decreasing runoff. The water diverted from flowing down the driveway and into storm drains
lessens the quantity of debris and other pollutants traveling with it, which stops it from pouring
into urban waterways. An extra benefit: Rainwater is also high in nitrogen, nature's fertilizer, so
it waters and feeds your landscape at the same time, free of charge.

Rainwater harvesting can be as simple as installing a rain barrel under a gutter coming off
the house. It can be expanded to include a cistern to handle overflow and to store the water
until you need it. A large system captures rainwater from more than one source. A home,
garage, and workshop can feed into one large underground cistern, and that water can then be
discharged via pump into a drip irrigation system.

## RAINWATER BARRELS

Collecting rainwater in barrels and tubs is the simplest way to begin using rainwater now. If you use a tub or open receptacle, use the water within 24 hours of collection. Open-water storage containers are a magnet for mosquitoes, the perfect environment for mold, and are accessible to rodents.

Rainwater barrels are easy to install and are readily available for purchase at most home-improvement centers. Look for barrels that have connecting devices that expand collection capacity by attaching to additional barrels. You can buy the barrels with all the parts necessary and installation instructions, or you can build it yourself as long as it meets these general criteria:

- The receptacle should hold least 50 gallons of water. Most manufactured rain barrels are 50- to 60-gallon capacity.
- Plastic is the preferred material as it is easy to keep clean.
- The barrel should be equipped with a child-resistant lid for safety and for keeping out pests. The lid should be removable so the barrel is accessible for cleaning.
- The intake opening should be fitted with a screen to minimize mosquito infestations and debris.
- There should be hardware to connect to the downspout on the home and a spigot for transferring water to a watering can and/or connecting to a hose.

Before installing the rain barrel, do a site inventory. You will need access to a downspout and a flat space to build a platform to elevate the barrel so the faucet accommodates a watering can or a space to attach a hose or drip line. The platform can be block, brick, wood, or concrete, but it needs to support the weight of the rain barrel when it is full of water. A 60-gallon barrel full of water weighs 450 pounds.

## CISTERNS

Cisterns are larger rainwater-holding receptacles that are installed above or below ground. They range in size from 100 gallons to thousands of gallons and are made from precast or reinforced concrete, fiberglass, cinder block and mortar, or steel. Cisterns require assistance from an architect and contractor for engineering and for installation. If most of your rainfall comes during the winter months and the water most likely won't be used until spring and summer, cisterns provide excellent long-term water storage. They may be installed aboveground, and if they are situated above the highest hose bib, they can be passively activated, with the water fed by gravity into a hose or drip line.

Continued on page 58

This rain barrel overflows with captured rain often in spring and summer, supplying water for container gardens and greenhouse plants. Water runoff from the swamp cooler in summer is captured in the barrel and waters a small postage stamp-sized lawn by connecting a soaker hose to the spigot.

WATER-SMART DESIGN SOLUTIONS

1 Select a location for the barrel under a downspout. Locate your barrel as close to the area you want to irrigate as possible. Make sure the barrel has a stable, level base. Connect the overflow tube, and make sure it is pointed away from the foundation.

2 Connect the spigot near the bottom of the barrel. Some kits may include a second spigot for filling watering cans. Use Teflon tape at all threaded fittings to ensure a tight seal. Remove the downspout, and set the barrel on its base.

3 Cut the downspout to length with a hacksaw. Reconnect the elbow fitting to the downspout using sheet metal screws. Attach the cover to the top of the rain barrel. Some systems include a cover with porous wire mesh, to which the downspout delivers water. Others include a cover with a sealed connection (next step).

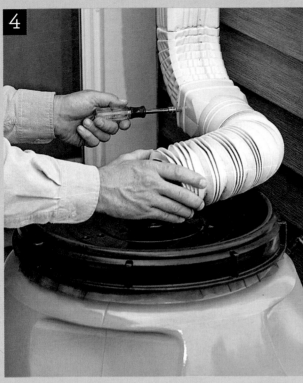

**4** Link the downspout elbow to the rain barrel with a length of flexible downspout extension attached to the elbow and the barrel cover.

Variation: If your barrel comes with a downspout adapter, cut away a segment of downspout and insert the adapter so it diverts water into the barrel.

**5** Connect a drip irrigation tube or garden hose to the spigot. A Y-fitting, such as the one shown here, will let you feed the drip irrigation system through a garden hose when the rain barrel is empty.

**6** If you want, increase water storage by connecting two or more rain barrels together with a linking kit, available from many kit suppliers.

Continued from page 55

If you live in colder climates, aboveground cisterns are subject to freezing. Waiting until the ice thaws in spring is an option if you don't need the water until then, but it does cause stress on the cistern that can lead to cracking. Installing a cistern underground provides a solution and situates it out of view, tucked under the house or deck, in an excavated site or in a basement. It requires a pump to move the water, which enables the cistern to work in tandem with an irrigation system.

Cisterns are basically closed systems, but require a bit of maintenance to keep them working smoothly. Keep the gutters and roof clean, free from overhanging branches and leaves that might slow down the flow of rainwater or clog it with debris. Cisterns, screens, and filters should be cleaned on an annual basis; an early spring check gets all in good working order in time for spring rains. Check the cistern at least twice a year for cracks or leaks. If the cistern is connected to a drip irrigation system, then maintain the drip systems by cleaning filters and checking for leaks, clogged emitters, and cracked drip tubing on a monthly basis. (See Water-Wise Watering, Chapter 4.)

Initiating water-smart design solutions makes the most out of water resources by directing the flow of water where it is needed through the use of berms and basins, swales, terraces, and drainage systems. Capturing and storing rainwater allows us to use less of our (usually limited) water budget in the landscape. Using the water so that it is of the most benefit to the plants and knowing *when* and *how* to water are techniques that create a healthy, water-smart garden.

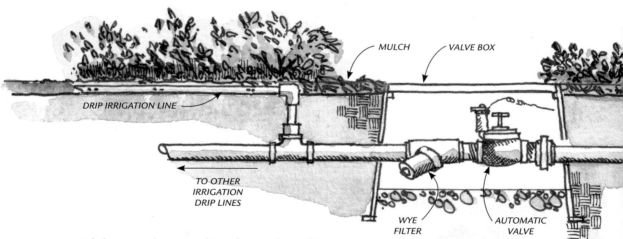

DRIP IRRIGATION LINE

MULCH    VALVE BOX

TO OTHER
IRRIGATION
DRIP LINES

WYE
FILTER

AUTOMATIC
VALVE

**A belowground storage cistern has a submersible pump in the bottom of the tank. The water is pumped out of the tank, passes through a valve and filter manifold, then moves through a delivery line that connects into the irrigation system.**

Two cisterns, approximately 600 gallons each and linked to each other, capture and store rainwater, which is then delivered by gravity to a drip irrigation system.

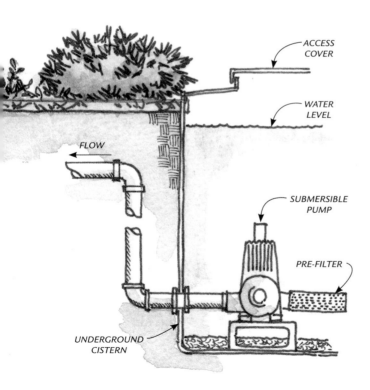

ACCESS COVER

WATER LEVEL

FLOW

SUBMERSIBLE PUMP

PRE-FILTER

UNDERGROUND CISTERN

Water-wise watering begins with selecting the irrigation system that directs the water where the plants need it by obtaining design assistance for system efficiency, and from utilizing new and cutting edge technologies focused on water-saving methods.

# Water-Wise Watering

**W**HEN THE TEMPERATURES HEAT up and the sun beats down, it is a common practice for many to take out the hose and water the garden. There is no doubt that it soothes our souls and cools us off as we lazily drift the water back and forth on the plants, watering leaves, soil, and our feet in unison. We figure if *we* are hot, then the plants must be hot, too. Our thoughts wander as we go about watering, thinking about how our day went and wondering what's for dinner. The water runs and we walk with hose in hand, making sure all is dripping wet before dragging it to another part of the yard.

Some fortunate homeowners find themselves gardening in a landscape with a professionally installed irrigation system, complete with timer, valves, underground and out-of-site mainlines, lateral lines, and drip tubing with emitters. Every morning, like clockwork, the heads magically pop up out of the lawn in unison and sparkling water settles on the blades, seeping into the soil. We hear just a hiss as the drip irrigation system is activated and find comfort in knowing that the water is slowly dripping out of the emitters, applying the water to the roots of a plant buried deeply under a thick layer of mulch.

The nursery label states if a plant is drought tolerant. It seems a perfect choice for the garden as we try to recover from skyrocketing water bills. It's a beauty, with its feathery gray-green foliage and brightly colored flowers. It's wondrous how such a lush and tropical-looking plant can be drought tolerant. At home, a hole is dug, the plant carefully set into the hole, and backfilled. Then it is watered thoroughly, foliage and all, until the little basin built around the stem is filled with water. As the water settles, a thick layer of mulch is applied to cool the soil and hold the water in. With all the proper steps followed, the plant is left to take care of itself, being the xeric plant that it is claimed to be. These scenarios seem quite idyllic, don't they?

# In the Real World

In the real world of water-wise watering, these scenarios all lead to increasingly high water bills, wilting plants, burned leaves, water running down the sidewalk, and the worst fate of all—failing plants.

Building a water-smart landscape takes time. It requires us to learn from the plants and the signals they send notifying us of when they need water. A well-designed and executed irrigation system can save water, time, and money giving plants the water they need where and when they need it. Like any other home system, it needs monitoring, maintenance, and repairs.

Drought-tolerant plants have characteristics that make them that way, but their water-saving advantages don't come into play until they are well-established, healthy, thriving plants. Small gardens, newly planted trees, container gardens, vegetable beds, and additions to the garden design are situations where hand-watering may make the most sense. Care must be taken in applying the water where the plants need it and only applying the amount required to do the job.

**Innovative technologies create sprinkler heads that are designed to apply water efficiently.**

Increased efforts in water conservation in the landscape, technological advances in irrigation system design, and research into old ways of watering modeled into new innovations help us be water-wise in our gardens. Having an understanding of how plants use water, recognizing the plant signals that tell us that they are thirsty, and then applying the water wisely will create a healthy, thriving, drought-tolerant, and beautiful garden.

# Plants and Their Signals

The diversity of plants means varied water requirements that differ from species to species. Some plants, such as large, leafy, lush, tropical-in-origin plants, always want a cool, moist soil and don't mind an occasional light mist on their leaves on a hot summer day. Other plants that grow naturally in arid regions need water applied deeply to reach their root systems, and they prefer the soil to dry out a bit between waterings. Still others, with shallow spreading roots, enjoy a quick spray of water that just barely wets a few inches of soil, simulating a summer rain. The challenge is knowing when and how to water. The answers lie in the plants and the signals they send.

**The frequency of watering varies with the maturity of the plants.** Seedlings and newly planted lawns require misting many times a day to avoid drying out leaves and delicate root systems. Container plants and vegetable gardens need watering each day throughout most of their lives. Newly transplanted shrubs and trees need slow, deep watering one to two times a week for three to six years until they are established.

**Watering regimens vary with the seasons.** Deciduous plants drop their leaves in the fall, and plants that go winter-dormant don't require any water during the winter, unless there is a prolonged period without water. Evergreens hold onto their leaves throughout the year, only shedding older foliage and slowing growth during the winter, so they require less water in fall

Container gardens dry out quickly as pots heat up in the sun and soil and air temperatures rise. Water containers daily, applying water slowly until it begins draining from the bottom of the pots. If summer temperatures are on the rise, move containers to a shadier location.

and winter. Many native plants experience their period of dormancy in the heat of the summer and need less water during that time.

**Plants show water stress in a number of ways.** When leaves lack water, they lose turgidity: the vascular system is restricted and leaves wilt. Most plants can regain their footing after wilting; once deeply watered they go on to good growing as if the deficit never occurred. Temporary wilting occurs on some plants that curl their leaves on a hot summer day (as with squash), a sort of plant reflex that reduces evapotranspiration and leaf surface exposure. As the night cools, the leaves unfurl.

**A change in foliage color is another sign of water stress.** Deep green leaves will lack luster and turn to lighter, pale green. Lawns turn a lighter shade of grayish green. When you walk on a water-stressed lawn, your footsteps will remain visible, embedded in the blades—a sign that the blades are losing turgidity. In drastic situations, old and new leaves on a water-stressed plant turn completely yellow and drop, which is the plant's last defense against lack of water before the roots desiccate and the entire plant dies.

But plants send out similar signals for other issues that might be at play. Wilting is also a sign of pests, rodent damage to the roots, and a waterlogged soil. Change of color in the leaves can be pests or nutrient deficiencies. The rule of thumb before you take any action is to bend down, put your finger in the soil, and *check the soil moisture first*. If the soil is dry down past the first joint in your index finger (it is a universal water gauge!), then apply water. If the soil is moist, then the signs are a warning that there are other issues.

How you apply the water is of equal importance. Plants take in a small amount of water from their leaf surfaces, but most of the action takes place in the soil, where the roots are the main player in absorbing water and transporting it through the vascular system up to the growing tips and leaves. When water is sprayed on the leaves on a hot day, the plant will absorb a bit of water from the leaves, but usually the heat and the sun speed up the evaporation so the

**Water the soil, not the plant leaves. Drip irrigation (Netafim, Inc.) directs the water where the plants need it.**

leaf tips actually burn in the process. While water may cool the plant down, it does not get the water where it needs it—to the roots—so the wilting still progresses. These two facts explain why it is important to water in the cooler early morning or late evening hours and to apply water to the soil, not the leaves. The cool temps allow the water to be absorbed into the soil when the evaporation rate is minimized: applying it to the soil puts the water where it is needed, avoiding leaf burn.

Watch the plants for warning signs that something is amiss. If they need water, then apply it slowly and deeply to the soil. If you let the plants and the soil be your watering guides, the watering choices you make will be wise ones.

# Watering New Plantings & Hardening Off Established Plants

It's no wonder plants go into transplant shock. They experience some surprise upon finding themselves uprooted from the pot or from another garden spot, and moved to an entirely new environment that may be sunnier, shadier, cooler, or warmer than where they were before. The very best way to get plants through this period and on their way to producing new roots and growth is to give them water—lots of water.

It may seem counterproductive to advocate using a lot of water when trying to create a water-wise garden. But even the most water-efficient plants need ample watering their first few years until they have established themselves with healthy, wide, and deep-reaching root systems that will make them drought tough for the rest of their lives. How long you need to keep up a strict watering regimen depends upon the type of plant, soil, and climate extremes. Applying water correctly when a plant needs it and using mulches to hold in moisture will establish a plant well in a short amount of time; then it will thrive for many years on natural rainfall, with minimal supplemental watering.

## WATERING TIPS FOR NEW PLANTINGS

Upon planting, water the soil surrounding and extending beyond the root zone of the plant. Lay a hose or soaker hose in the area and allow water to trickle slowly into the soil. Lawns and meadows are best watered overhead for good coverage, either by activating the irrigation system, hand-watering, or by portable sprinkler in small sections at a time.

The water should percolate down into the soil beyond the root zone of the plant. It may take a few waterings to fill the basins of trees and shrubs (see Chapter 7 for planting guidelines), depending upon the soil type and the moisture level of the soil when you planted. Lawns and meadows may need repeated short periods of watering to avoid water runoff. This initial watering is important to seal the soil around the roots and to provide the moisture roots need to begin rejuvenation.

Maintain consistently moist but not soggy soil for the first couple of weeks after planting. Then begin spacing the watering to every few days, allowing the soil to dry to just one inch deep before watering again. Maintain this regimen for landscape plants for a few more weeks, then begin tapering off watering to twice weekly for the rest of the first season, as long as the plant is not showing signs of water stress. Lawns and meadows should not be allowed to dry out between watering until they are germinated and have good root development. Four to six weeks after sodding or sowing, taper off the watering for the remainder of the season, watering twice weekly through the heat of summer.

The just plug-planted meadow in the foreground will require short, regular waterings from overhead until the plugs establish and show signs of new growth. The established meadow grasses in the background have been gradually weaned off supplemental watering, surviving and thriving on natural rainfall.

# CHAPTER 4

## HARDENING OFF ESTABLISHED PLANTS

Upon establishment, water plants on an "as needed" basis. This may mean supplemental deep watering during long periods without rain and extended high summer temps. Watch the plants carefully for wilting or color change and check the soil before you water. Apply water very deeply to accommodate mature root systems extending beyond the drip lines.

Watering in spring and fall should be on an as-needed basis. The following chart is a guideline for summer watering regimens (when they need the most water) for plants until they are established.

| Plant type | 2nd Summer | 3rd Summer | 4th Summer | 5th Summer | 6th Summer |
|---|---|---|---|---|---|
| Lawns | 2x/week | 1x/week | 1x/week | 1x/week | 1x/week |
| Meadows | 1x/week | 1x/week | 2x/month | 1x/month | As needed |
| Trees* | 3x/week | 2x/week | 1x/week | 2x/month | 1x/month |
| Shrubs | 2x/week | 1x/week | 2x/month | 1x/month | As needed |

*Trees are established in the seventh summer. Water as needed.

This meadow planting includes mature grasses, perennials, trees, and shrubs that all survive and thrive with minimal supplemental watering in extended periods of no rainfall.

# Choosing the Right System for Your Needs

Hand-watering your entire landscape is painstaking work, requiring constant monitoring to make sure you are getting good coverage by moving the hose or sprinkler often before the water starts running down the sidewalk. If your lawn or bed space is larger than 400 square feet, dragging a sprinkler or watering with a hose is impractical, takes *a lot* of time, and is inefficient in minimizing runoff or getting complete coverage.

Irrigation systems, when properly designed, bring a level of control over when and how you apply water, then apply it evenly and in increments that allow the water to percolate in to the soil, minimizing runoff. Today's irrigation systems blend best watering practices with new technologies to create a water-conserving/water-smart method for watering the landscape. Most home landscapes will require both sprinkler and drip irrigation systems to accommodate their needs.

In my garden, I use sprinkler irrigation on lawns and meadows. Shrubs, flowerbeds, vegetables and fruits, vines, groundcovers, and bulbs are watered by drip irrigation. Properly designed sprinkler systems apply the amount of water needed by the plants, exactly where and when it is needed, and evenly distribute water to the entire area, while minimizing loss of water through overspray or runoff.

## SPRINKLER IRRIGATION

An overhead or sprinkler irrigation system is the best method for watering flat surfaces that are home to lawns, meadow grasses, and native plants that have shallower root systems. Most sprinklers, developed for today's water-conscience landscape, put out a low volume of water (measured by the number of gallons of water emitted in one minute—that is, gpm) and are designed with special water-saving traits.

Some sprinkler heads have built-in pressure regulators to adjust the water pressure to the optimum level for discharging water. There are low or angled nozzles with adjustable patterns for watering irregular shaped spaces. Precision spray heads are designed for patio or small garden beds, efficiently watering narrow spaces just 30 inches wide. With all the flexibility and options, there is a sprinkler irrigation system to efficiently water any area, large or small.

Sprinkler irrigation systems apply water from overhead using water that is transported through underground pipes connected to the mainline. At the point of connection is a manifold (comprised of a backflow prevention device), a pressure regulator, and a series of valves that distribute the water to lateral lines. Then the water moves to the risers that hold the sprinkler heads. Sprinkler heads have two varieties: pop up (for lawns and meadows) or stationary for landscape beds. In an automatic irrigation system, the valves are located closer to the zone of plants they are watering, with wires that run below ground connecting to a central irrigation control clock or timer, safely located in the garage or inside the home. The valves are activated by the timer or can be run manually by flipping a switch located on the valve.

Spray systems require knowledge of system hydraulics, soil structure, and plant needs. There is a bit of cash output involved, but having a properly designed system will save water and keep your landscape thriving for years to come. Defer analyzing your site and designing your system to professionals, or take classes in system hydraulics and design at local universities or online to do it yourself.

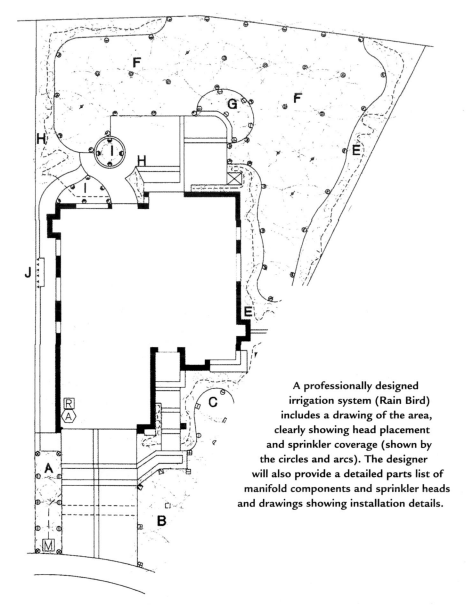

A professionally designed irrigation system (Rain Bird) includes a drawing of the area, clearly showing head placement and sprinkler coverage (shown by the circles and arcs). The designer will also provide a detailed parts list of manifold components and sprinkler heads and drawings showing installation details.

Your irrigation designer should provide you with a drawn-to-scale plan showing pipe sizing and layout from the mainline to the valve and to the plant zones. The selected sprinkler heads and manifold components will be noted on the plan, listing manufacturer, model number, and any other specifications. Supplemental detail drawings should be provided that clearly illustrate manifold construction, sprinkler head/riser installation, and, if the system is automated, wiring details.

After the plan is completed, you can do the labor and installation of the system yourself to save money, as long as you follow the plan to exact specifications. Installation will require a fair amount of trenching, so renting a trencher will be in order, followed by handwork with a shovel. You will need to be able to work on your knees while gluing pipe and installing risers and sprinkler heads. Do a final system check for leaks, then backfill the trenches before installing the landscape.

This sprinkler system consists of low volume, rotator sprinkler heads (Hunter Irrigation) that distribute the water evenly to the entire lawn, giving head-to-head coverage for a healthy turf with no dry spots. The watering pattern and droplet size minimize overspray, conserving water.

---

If you hire a contractor to install the system, request that an "as-built" be provided. While the plan should be followed exactly as designed, there are always surprises found underground that may cause re-routing of lateral lines, adjustments in spacing, quantity of heads, or altering the location of valves. An as-built will clearly show any changes on the plan. Request a final walk-through inspection from the contractor while the system is running to make sure all is in working order. Get a briefing on valve and component locations, system operation and maintenance procedures, and if the system is automated, a training session for timer mechanics and irrigation scheduling.

An investment of this size requires maintenance. Sprinkler systems should be checked once each week, while they are running, for:

· clogged nozzles that stop or slow the flow of water or deter the head from
   properly activating
· bubbling water or geysers that signal a broken riser or pipe, or a damaged
   head or nozzle
· spray patterns that are disrupted or askew, not distributing water evenly,
   or throwing water out of the irrigated space

In order to keep the system running efficiently, always replace nozzles or sprinkler heads with the exact model/nozzle as the design specified. If you deviate at all, replacing the broken head with any other make, model, or type of head, the replacement creates an imbalance of water distribution, system inefficiency, and ultimately, plant water stress and plant loss.

Keep an eye on plants in the landscape for signs of stress and for dry spots. With a properly designed system, you can be confident that the plants will be thriving, but check the landscape regularly for telltale signs. It's best not to wait for the plants to send the signals that they are water stressed. If they have severe wilt, then even after repairing the irrigation, they may not regain vigor, and you have lost the plant.

1 Tap into your water supply. Shut off the water at the main shutoff valve. On the downstream side of your water meter, install a compression T-fitting. To supply the irrigation system, you will need to run PVC pipe to the manifold location. At a convenient location inside the house, install a gate valve with bleed in the line. Outside, dig a 10-in. trench leading to the manifold location. Drill a 1-in. hole through the sill directly above the trench, and route the pipe through the hole and down to the trench using an L-fitting. You may also need to install a backflow prevention or an anti-siphon device between the main and the irrigation manifold; check local codes.

2 Choose a manifold with as many outlets as you have zones. The manifold shown here has two zones. Assemble the manifold as directed (some come preassembled, others are solvent-glued) and set it in the hole. Connect the supply pipe from the house to the manifold with an automated control module. Install the controller on the house near the supply pipe and run the included wires under the supply pipe from the valves to the control module.

3 Use stakes or landscape flags to mark the sprinkler locations, and then mark the pipe routes with spray paint or string. Once all the locations are marked, dig the trenches. In nonfreezing climates, trenches can be as little as 6 in. In freezing climates, dig trenches at least 10 in. deep. Renting a trencher can speed the job considerably. Set the sod aside so you can replace it after the sprinklers are installed.

4 Lay the pipe. Work on one zone at a time, beginning at the manifold. Connect the first section of PVC or PE pipe (PE shown) to the manifold outlet with solvent glue for PVC, or a barbed coupler and pipe clamps for PE (shown). At the first sprinkler location, connect a T-fitting with a female-threaded outlet for the riser. Continue with the next run of pipe to the next sprinkler location. Install T-fittings at each sprinkler location. At the end of each zone, install an L-fitting for the last sprinkler.

5 Install the risers for the sprinkler heads. Risers come in a variety of styles. The simplest are short, threaded pipe nipples, but flexible and cut-to-fit risers are also available. Use a riser recommended by the manufacturer for your sprinkler head. For pop-up heads, make sure the nipple is the correct length for proper sprinkler operation.

6 Once all the risers are in place, flush the system. Turn on the water and open the valves for each zone one at a time, allowing the water to run for about a minute or until it runs clear. After the system is flushed, begin installing the sprinkler heads. Thread the heads onto the risers and secure them in place with earth. Make sure the heads are vertical (stake the risers if necessary). Fill in the rest of the trenches and replace the sod.

Variation: In freezing climates, it's a good idea to install a valve with a fitting that allows the system to be drained with compressed air. Install the fitting downstream of any antisiphon valves but before the manifold. In the fall, close the irrigation system's shutoff valve and open any drain valves. At the manifold, open one zone's valve and blow air into the zone until no water comes out. Repeat for each zone.

WATER-WISE WATERING

Left: **Drip irrigation tubing (Netafim Ltd.) is laid out on a steep slope. The water will drip slowly from the inline emitters, applying water to the roots of the plants where they need it and with minimal runoff.**
Right: **Drip irrigation tubing with inline emitters (Netafim Ltd.) applies water evenly, deeply, and slowly to this shrub bed. The bed can be intensively planted with drought-tolerant trees, shrubs, and groundcovers, all on the same hydrozone and valve.**

## DRIP IRRIGATION

Drip irrigation delivers water directly to the soil, providing a slow drip of water. The water is directed to the roots of the plant where it needs it, with minimal to no loss of water through overspray, evaporation, or runoff. Sloped areas, terraced and raised beds, landscaped areas, and container gardens are all best watered using drip irrigation. Trees, shrubs, annuals, perennials, bulbs, fruit and vegetable crops, orchards, groundcovers, cacti, and succulents have deep- and wide-reaching root systems, so providing water directly to their roots makes water immediately available to the plants, avoiding water stress and encouraging root system growth, contributing to a healthy drought-tough landscape.

A drip irrigation system connects to an underground lateral line that runs off the main water line. A drip system manifold consists of the valve, pressure regulator, and a filter. The pressure required to activate a drip system is very low, so a pressure regulator turns the pressure down to fulfill system requirements, while protecting the tubing from splitting or from emitters blowing out from the force of water. Due to the slower flow of water, a filter diminishes the soil particulates and debris that can easily clog a valve, drip line, or emitter. From the valve, a length of underground PVC pipe delivers water to the zone, then drip tubing is attached and laid upon the surface of the soil. The drip tubing delivers water through an emitter that discharges the water. Usually, the drip lines are covered with a layer of mulch.

Emitters discharge water at a rate calculated by the number of gallons of water emitted in one hour (gallons per hour, or gph) and range from 1 gph to 6 gph. Due to this slow discharge, drip systems often run for hours, depending upon the soil type and the plant

The use of a soaker hose around this peach tree shows placement of the hose to thoroughly water the entire root system. Roots extend far beyond the drip line as trees mature. Slow, deep watering ensures good root development.

water requirements. There are emitters that drip the water onto the soil and emitters that send out the same low amount of water, but deliver it as a fine, small spray (spot spitters or micro-spray emitters). They are inserted directly into the tubing or into the end of smaller tubing (called spaghetti- or micro-tubing), which is anchored to the soil at the base of a plant or into the landscape bed. A drip system commonly used in agricultural and vegetable garden settings, in-line emitters are embedded into tubing at 8-, 12-, 18-, or 24-inch spacing.

Drip irrigation systems are a bit easier to design yourself if you have the infrastructure of underground pipes to deliver the water. The system and manifold components are homeowner friendly in providing detailed instructions for designing the system to your landscape, laying out the lines, placing emitters, securing the tubing, and making adjustments. Because the drip lines run along the soil surface, there is no trenching unless you want to bury the lines out of site, which requires just hand trenching down a few inches deep. The tubing splices together using compression or clamp fittings, so no gluing is required. You can install the system before or after you plant, retrofit a spray system to drip, and accommodate growing root systems by adding tubing or emitters as the plants grow.

Drip irrigation systems need your diligence regarding system checks, repairs, and manifold maintenance. Because the water moves so slowly, particulates can easily clog tubing or emitters. If this happens, then the first sign that something is amiss will be wilting plants. It may be too late for the plant even if you make the repairs at that point. So walk the lines and do random close-up viewing of the emitters in action while the system is running; check the plants daily during the heat of summer. Other drip irrigation system checks are:

· At the ends of each run of drip line, the hose is either clamped or crimped. An occasional flush of water through the system with the end caps removed cleans out the tubing.

- Service the filter. The bottom portion has an outlet with an open/close valve. Every month, open the valve, turn on the water, and let it pour freely out of the outlet. This flushes out particulates captured in the filter. Each spring, unscrew the bottom portion of the filter, remove the screen, hose it off, give it a few taps, and replace.
- If tubing punctures, cracks, breaks, or crimps, cut off the flow of water to emitters and plants downstream, then repair immediately. When you purchase the system components and tubing, buy extra couplings, end caps, tees, elbows and goof plugs (yes, they are called that!) that fit the tubing you buy, so you are ready for repairs.

## MANUAL WATERING

The one-acre landscape at my home has an automated irrigation system that includes both sprinkler and drip applications that water turf, landscape, orchards, vineyard, flowering annuals and perennials, bulb beds, meadows, and vegetable gardens. Even with all of those on a programmed timer, I still pick up a hose almost daily for manual hand watering. Sprinklers, soaker hoses, hose-end connecting irrigation tape, and hose-bib connecting drip systems are all types of manual watering. The good news is that we can control the flow, direct it exactly where we need it, and then move it to another spot in the garden. The bad news is that it's easy to waste water, diminishing our water conservation efforts in the landscape.

If you have a postage-stamp landscape, then hand watering might be your only source of watering, making water conservation a difficult, though not impossible, task. Maintain control over hand watering: be water-smart by selecting the right watering tools to use for the job, and only apply as much water as needed to maintain healthy plants while minimizing runoff. Before

Left: **Lawn sprinklers should be adjusted to avoid overspray and misting. Turn the flow down to water small areas at a time, moving the sprinkler as soon as the water starts to run off the area.**

Middle: **A watering wand extends the reach; the water breaker allows you to stop the flow while moving from place to place; the nozzle puts out large droplets of water in an even pattern.**

Right: **This irrigation timer (compliments of The Toro Company) is state-of-the-art, but homeowner user-friendly, controlling up to eight zones/valves with the aid of a wireless weather sensor. Program the timer just once, and the timer software automatically adjusts watering times to fluctuating temperatures and rainfall.**

watering, watch a plant for signs that it *needs* water, then check the soil with your fingers to make sure it is dry. Apply the water to the soil, allowing it to percolate deeply into the soil to reach the root zone of the plant.

**Hose:** Add a water-breaker and a nozzle to the hose before watering container gardens, new plantings, plants that need an extra drink during a dry spell, seed beds, and small landscaped areas. The water breaker allows you to turn the water on and off when moving from plant to plant and slows the flow to a drip or a trickle, useful for filling tree and shrub basins. The nozzle maintains an even flow of water, which is applied in larger droplets, rather than a hard spray that evaporates quickly and pummels the soil and the plants.

**Sprinklers:** For irregularly shaped small lawns, use sprinklers with adjustable spray patterns to minimize overspray. Rather than try to water the entire area at once, use a lower flow that creates larger droplets and move the sprinkler a couple of times, making sure the watering pattern overlaps with each move so no spots are missed. When you see water running out of the area, turn the sprinkler off, and if more water is needed to penetrate beyond the roots, wait for the water to percolate into the soil, then run the water again.

**Soaker hoses and irrigation tape:** Soaker hoses put out quite a bit of water, and they put it out along the entire length of hose. Irrigation tape has holes in it, spaced equally apart along the entire length of tape, and it doesn't put out as much water as a soaker hose. For maximum coverage in large areas, lay the hose or tape out in a small section in large loops running alongside each other. If you are using it for tree or shrub basin watering, wrap it around the plant, beginning the loop outside the berm and working it in a circular fashion around the tree, ending next to the trunk. Turn the water on just enough for water to seep out of the hose or tape, then monitor it closely, turning it off when you see the water seeping out of the area. Move the hose to another spot, water there, then move it back to the original site, watering again until runoff occurs. Repeat until the entire soil profile is deeply watered

# Innovative Technologies

Technological advances in irrigation, soil science, and crop efficiency data make it possible for water-smart irrigation timers to take the guesswork out of deciding when to water and how much to apply for optimum plant health. The amount of water to apply is based upon the geographical location (your zip code), type of plants grown, how densely the area is planted, soil texture, historical weather data, and the evapotranspiration rate (ET), which is the sum of how much water the plant uses and how much is lost through evaporation. All this information is stored in the timer's computer database and compiled to determine how much to water the plants. In the event of power failure, the controller safely stores all the data and the irrigation program.

Irrigation timers are electric or battery- or solar-powered and come in 8-, 10-, 12-, and 24-station capacities. Larger and more complex timers are interactive systems used commercially to water huge landscape projects. When selecting a timer for home use, the stations directly relate to the number of valves or zones. Individual valves/stations are required for turf, trees, shrubs, slopes, vegetable gardens, orchards, and succulents. Sprinkler systems should never share a valve with drip systems. Lawns should have their own zone or zones depending upon the size. Add one or two additional stations for future landscape changes and expansion.

If it rains or the ground freezes, there are wireless sensors that can send the message to the timer to not run that day. There are also rotor sprinkler heads that run for short periods with pause intervals that allow the water to percolate into slow-draining soils before putting out more water. Innovative technology gives us cutting-edge tools, equipment, and methods all focused on creating a water-smart landscape.

## IRRIGATION SCHEDULING

Irrigation timers must be programmed to change with the seasons. As plants slow growth in the winter, they need less water or don't need any at all unless there is a long dry spell. In the spring, growth speeds up with rising air and soil temps. More water is needed, but the still cool soil needs to dry out between watering. In areas of late season frosts, it is important not to accelerate growth too much in early spring, as tender growth is susceptible to late frost damage. Summer temps may bring on monsoon rains, so systems need to be adjusted for infrequent downpours.

Irrigation timers should be monitored and the programs adjusted every three or four months, either by the homeowner or by the landscape maintenance technician. Run times will need to be adjusted to accommodate your soil type and climate variables, the maturity of the landscape, and fluctuating seasonal changes. If timers are electric, then power outages affect the schedule. Once the power comes back on, the time of day needs to be adjusted. Computer-based clocks usually will maintain data, but periodically check to make sure all is running properly. Activate the zone at the timer and do a visual check of the system while it is running. Then modify the run days, start time, and duration for each zone based upon the season, changing climate, and maturity of the plants.

## SEEP TECHNOLOGIES

Seep irrigation is not a new practice. Studies were conducted on methods of seep irrigation as long ago as 1890, when a revegetation project in the Sonoran desert tried various applications on new seedling growth for desert revegetation. Seep irrigation does what it sounds like: water is delivered directly to the root zone of the plant where it seeps into the soil profile. It is similar to the theory and application of a drip irrigation system, but seep irrigation methods do not require water pressure and are not susceptible to clogged lines and emitters.

A more recent study, conducted by the Soil Ecology & Restoration Group (SERG) and led by David A. Bainbridge of the Environmental Studies Program, U.S. International University, San Diego, California, shows two of the four methods reviewed, deep pipe and buried clay pot irrigation, are noteworthy for home landscapes. They are very DIY-friendly, inexpensive, and produce healthy, deep-rooted, well-established, drought-tolerant plants with minimal labor and construction.

## DEEP PIPE IRRIGATION

Deep pipe irrigation uses a length of pipe; PVC was used in studies—measuring ½- to 2 inches in diameter—with 1-mm holes drilled into it up and down the length, and a cap attached to one pipe end. The open pipe or pipes are inserted vertically into the ground, 12 to 18 inches deep, either on opposite sides of a tree basin or randomly into a garden bed. A screen is firmly attached to the top of the exposed pipe lip, which keeps out debris, insects, and rodents. Water is manually poured into the tube(s) or it can be delivered by means of a drip line. The water is dispersed out the holes in the pipe, and by means of capillary action it moves through the soil profile, where the nearby roots have easy access. The benefits sited for using deep pipe irrigation are:

- Can be used with low-quality water—
  no clogged lines or emitters
- Easy to build and install
- Water is delivered deeply into the soil with
  no evaporation or runoff
- Continued use creates a deeper, stronger
  root system, enabling established plants
  to survive drought

## BURIED CLAY POT IRRIGATION

Buried clay pot irrigation is a traditional method
enjoying a resurgence. An unfired clay pot is buried into
the ground in a tree or shrub basin or intermittently
throughout a landscape bed. The bottom hole has
been plugged using a silicone caulk. A tight-fitting
screen is attached securely to the top to keep out
debris and animals. The pot is filled, either manually
or by drip irrigation tubing, and the water seeps out of
the porous pot slowly into the soil profile. The benefits
cited for using buried clay pot irrigation are:

Irrigation solution: A series of buried
clay pots in the home landscape.
Screens keep out debris and animals.

- Easy to install and lasts for years
- No water pressure required
- The pots can hold water for a week or longer,
  depending upon your soil type, and can utilize rainwater
- The slow, steady release of water encourages strong, deep root formation

## RAINWATER HARVESTING

Though it may be familiar to some of us, rainwater harvesting is just beginning widespread
implementation in the U.S. Already widely used in Europe and Australia, it is still very new to
landscape applications here. (See Chapter 3 for more details on rainwater harvesting, including
DIY steps on installing a rain barrel.)

Water-wise watering begins as soon as you install a plant in the ground. Applying ample
water immediately after planting and continuing with a regular watering regimen throughout
the seasons creates healthy, drought-tolerant, mature plants with deep and far-reaching root
systems. Watching plants for signs of water stress, especially during the heat of summer, and
adjusting the irrigation system to the change with the season, maintains plant vigor through
the most challenging time of year. Well-designed sprinkler and drip irrigation systems
apply the proper amount of water when the plants need it, taking the guess work out of
determining a regular watering regimen. Using new technologies blended with tried-and-true
methods are valuable tools to apply water wisely in the home landscape.

There has been a bit of push in the industry of late to improve underground and subterrain
drip irrigation for turf, but there are still too many variables for it to be practical or applicable
at this time. While there are other technologies on the horizon that are concerned with
irrigation systems, timers, and sprinkler heads, they have not been tested enough to be proven
and considered in landscape situations—yet.

A soil display at Conservation Garden Park in West Jordan, Utah, illustrates the many different layers of soil. The top layer represents the organic layer, sometimes referred to as topsoil. Larger particles, stones, and other deposits formed from the parent material form an undulating pattern.

# Water-Conserving Solutions

**S**OMETIMES IT'S GOOD to recap what you know—you now have an understanding of how plants absorb water, so you know to water the roots and not the leaves. You know to watch the plants for signs of water stress and to check the soil before watering. And you know, in order to conserve water in the landscape for years to come, to provide deep and slow watering to nurture plants until they are established, when their deep and far-reaching healthy root systems allow them to survive on what nature provides.

But all of these water-wise methods become challenges if the soil in your landscape doesn't do its job. The soil needs to serve as a reservoir for the water, yet have air spaces for the water to move throughout the soil profile. Do you observe any of these things? Maybe as you water, the water just sits in a puddle, not percolating down in the soil at all. You fill a hole with water in preparation of planting, return after an hour and the water is still there. Or as you water, the water is absorbed into the soil, disappearing so fast, it's as if you never watered at all.

Effective water-conserving solutions build healthy soils at the same time. The building blocks for creating healthy soils are:

- Incorporate organic amendments to increase drainage and encourage microbe population, thereby contributing to soil fertility.
- Apply a thick layer of mulch to cool the soil and the roots, to hold in moisture, and to slow evaporation.
- Use microclimates that exist in patches of shade under tree canopies, on the north side of buildings, and under house overhangs; create microclimates with arbors, fences, and green screens.

- Grow water-thrifty plants that have similar needs together or in combination with edible crops to share water and soil resources. Two or more edible crops interplanted in the same space stretch the water budget and provide food for the table.
- Make the most out of the soil you have in your backyard by improving the texture, enhancing the soil structure, conserving moisture, and choosing plants that share the resources that go towards creating healthy, water-conserving landscapes.

# Building Healthy Soils

In our goal to have a healthy, water-smart landscape, water needs to be available to the plants, but with minimal waste. A well-draining soil is a key factor in how well water moves throughout the soil profile so the roots can use it, and then allows it to move beyond the area, removing salts with it. The soil texture dictates the amount of air spaces available for water movement.

Soils are made up of a combination of sand, silt, and clay. Sand contains the largest particles of the three; they are round and lack structure. If you wet a pile of sand and make a ball with it, the water evaporates quickly and the ball falls apart. Silt may have been sand at one time, but through weathering and decomposition, it becomes very smooth, similar to what is in the bottom of a streambed. Silt has a bit more structure than sand, but not much. Clay makes up the smallest soil particles, and these are more plate-like in structure. Clay also carries a negative electrical charge, which allows it to attract and hold water molecules. A little bit of clay is a good thing. A lot of clay holds onto the water so tightly that it doesn't give it up to the plants. When you have a soil that is heavy in clay and you make a ball, it will form a sticky mass, taking days to dry out, and even then, it maintains its shape.

Soil texture is determined by the amounts of sand, silt, and clay and their proportion to one another. The perfect soil is a loamy, well-balanced combination of sand (40 percent), silt (38 percent), and clay (22 percent). The sand and silt make up the most of the soil: sand provides air spaces and contributes to good drainage, while the silt allows the soil to absorb the water long enough for it to be taken up by the plants. The small amount of clay holds organic matter and carries a charge, allowing the water to be absorbed slowly, carrying nutrients with it.

To get an estimate of the proportions of sand, silt, and clay in your soil, you can perform a simple sedimentation test. Large heavy sand and silt particles will settle most rapidly in water, while small light clay particles settle slowly. Calgon laundry powder is used to dissolve the soil aggregates and keep the individual particles separated.

## SOIL SEDIMENTATION TEST

### MATERIALS

- Soil sample
- One quart fruit jar with lid
- 8 percent Calgon solution (mix 6 tablespoons of Calgon (a laundry powder available in stores) per 1 quart of water)
- Metric ruler
- Measuring cup
- Tablespoon

### PROCEDURE

1. Place about ½ cup of soil in the jar. Add 3½ cups water and 5 tablespoons Calgon solution.
2. Cap the jar and shake for 5 minutes. Let settle for 24 hours.
3. After 24 hours, measure the depth of settled soil. All soil particles have settled, so this is the Total Depth. Write down the measurement.

4. Shake for another 5 minutes. Let stand 40 seconds. The sand will settle out quickly. Measure the depth of the settled soil only and record the measurement as Sand Depth.

5. Do not shake again. Let the jar stand for another 30 minutes. Measure the depth again, and subtract the sand depth to get the Silt Depth, which will be a bit darker in color than the sand.

6. The remaining unsettled particles are clay, lighter in color than the silt, and they will be on top.

Subtract Silt and Sand Depth from Total Depth to get Clay Depth.

7. Now calculate the percentage of each soil separate using these formulas:

$$\% \text{ sand} = \frac{\text{sand depth} \times 100}{\text{total depth}}$$

$$\% \text{ silt} = \frac{\text{silt depth} \times 100}{\text{total depth}}$$

$$\% \text{ clay} = \frac{\text{clay depth} \times 100}{\text{total depth}}$$

Find your estimated percentages on the texture triangle to determine your soil texture. If you suspect that the texture of your soil differs from site to site around your property, then perform individual sedimentation tests accordingly.

Most of us *don't* have the perfect loam soil in our landscapes. During the home construction process, soils are removed, stored in piles, churned up, and redistributed after the home is built, leading to a mix of soil quite different from what was there before construction. All the moving and churning affects the texture of your soil. Soil pH remains fairly constant and relates to soil

**Each side of the texture triangle is a sand, silt, or clay soil particle. Note the percentage of your sedimentation findings for each corresponding particle. The point where the three percentages intersect tells the texture of your soil.**

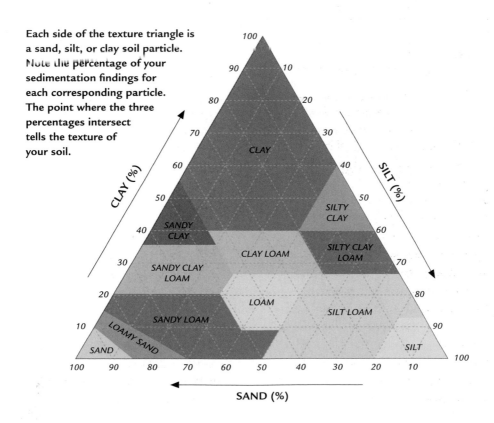

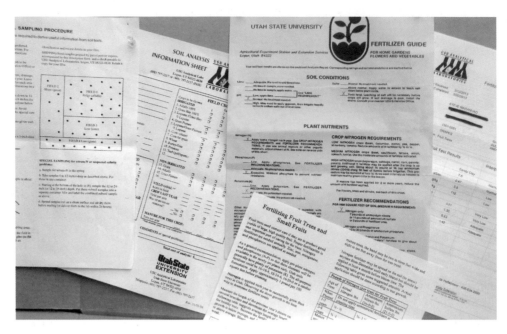

**Soil sample results from the Cooperative Extension list soil analysis, recommendations for soil treatments, supplemental fertilizers, and additional specific crop information pertinent to the area and climate.**

minerals and nutrients, climate/weather patterns, and amount of rainfall. It's important to know your soil pH, texture, and the amount of nutrients present in the soil before applying any supplements or amendments.

A soil test will report soil pH, confirm its texture, and indicate the presence or lack of nutrients. Nutrient deficiencies will be accompanied by recommendations for fertilizer applications. Recommendations from the soil test might include incorporating lime or gypsum if the soil is *highly* acidic or alkaline. These should never be added unless they are recommended by an extension agent or testing lab. Self-diagnosing can lead to additional problems. Soil pH can only be adjusted for short periods; there is no permanent way to change the pH of the soil. It is more practical to match the plant with your pH.

Soil fertility is key to good plant growth. If the soil texture does not allow good water movement, then added nutrients will not be available to the plants. It would take enormous quantities of materials to change the texture of soil, but you *can* improve it at planting time to give young roots a well-draining soil to grow in and to create a favorable environment for new root growth. Incorporating organic amendments on a seasonal basis builds soil fertility and improves drainage. For established plantings, use organic mulch, or top-dress with organics and apply water to build the soil and to increase drainage over long periods.

Incorporating amendments is the optimum treatment for poorly draining soils, whether they're sandy, clayey, or rocky. Amendments added at the time of planting should be mixed into the existing soil before backfilling. When importing topsoil for the landscape, it too should be thoroughly incorporated with the existing soil. This process avoids interfacing, which is essentially the point where the topsoil meets the existing soil, acting as a barrier and blocking water passage and plant roots.

## ORGANIC AMENDMENTS AND SOIL CONDITIONERS

When we refer to adding organics to the soil, compost comes to mind. At my home, we have four compost bins because we make our own from layering kitchen scraps, soil, and green waste, but it is never enough for all the garden spaces. It gets divided up and added to alternate beds each season. Properly layered, stirred occasionally, and watered, a good compost pile can churn out rich "black gold" teeming with earthworms every three months or so.

### COMPOST: "BLACK GOLD"

You can make your own compost in a system you build yourself, or you can purchase a compost bin that allows easy turning and mixing. An enclosed bin generates the internal heat needed to speed up the decomposition, holds in moisture, and keeps the mix free from rodents and insects. Bagged compost is also available at the garden center. A good rule of thumb is to spread a 3-inch layer of compost over the entire area you are amending, then incorporate that before planting.

Compost is high in nutrients, including large amounts of phosphorus, nitrogen, potassium, and calcium. The added bonuses are the earthworms and microbes that occur in a "well cooked" compost. Microbes occur naturally in all soils and in high numbers. You cannot see them, but under a microscope, bacteria, fungi, nematodes, and protozoa form a vast microbe network, generally congregating around the root systems of plants.

A teaspoon of good garden compost contains *thousands* of protozoa, miles of fungal hyphae if they were stretched out of their weblike structure, billions of bacteria, and dozens of nematodes. Singly, some of the microbes can do some damage. Fungal disease can collapse a root system

---

The essential elements for making compost: water, kitchen scraps (no meat or proteins), and brown and green waste. The piles are turned by rotating between the two bins, which adds airspace to the mix and churns it up to accelerate decomposition, and water is added to keep the pile moist.

quicker than invading nematodes. Yet living together in the right numbers, the fungi surrounding the roots of a plant can trap a nematode, thwarting its efforts to penetrate plant roots.

In a well-populated, balanced microbial soil, plants are naturally healthy, disease- and pest-free. If one population is destroyed or limited in reproduction, losing its place in the soil food chain, then the balance is off and the effects can be difficult to reverse. Pesticides kill naturally occurring microbes, and it takes years to repeated incorporation of organics to repair the balance. Overtilling also disrupts the delicate balance, dispersing the microbes and requiring time for the web to rebuild.

## OTHER ORGANICS

**Mycorrhizae fungi** contribute to overall plant growth, build tolerance to high saline levels, assist recovery from transplant shock, aid root establishment, and increase resistance to plant diseases and the effects of drought. In undisturbed areas, the high numbers of mycorrhizae are credited for the lack of root diseases. Healthy soils are soils rich in microbes, which affect the texture and structure of the soil. When you incorporate compost into soil, you are giving a healthy dose of nutrients and soil microbes all at once.

Other organics also include **animal manures and peat moss**. Manures should be used only *after* they have been "cured" or broken down a bit. Bagged or bulk quantities of manures should be laid in shallow piles in the sun to decompose further and be watered, as they are very high in salts. Then incorporate the cured manures into the soil and water deeply to further leach salts before planting. Leaching is done by watering an area to a depth of 10 to 12 inches. In slow-draining soils, this may mean watering to the point of puddling, waiting for the water to penetrate, then applying water again, repeating the process until the needed water depth is achieved. Leaching moves the salts below and beyond the plant root zones. Seasonally leaching the soil is necessary where compost is used regularly.

Though peat moss has a bit of nutrient value and is acidic, it's mostly used for its ability to hold water. It can increase water-holding capacity for sandy soils: if it is well worked, fluffed up, and incorporated into the existing soil, it can improve airspace and drainage.

## SOIL CONDITIONERS IMPROVE DRAINAGE

Soil conditioners may include a number of elements that assist in drainage or water absorption. Organic soil conditioners are of the most benefit since they may contribute to the microbial activity and usually try to mimic the improvements that come from organic amending. Humus-based products contain from 30 to 60 percent of humic acids and additional nutrients.

**Green crops** include nitrogen-rich plants such as clovers, vetch, and legumes. Seed an area in fall for overwintering and for germination in very early spring, or sow in early spring, as soon as the ground can be worked, for germination by mid-spring. Farmers that green crop rototill, or plow the plants under before they flower to increase nutrients and soil drainage. In a small garden application, they can be turned into the soil by shovel to avoid compaction or overtilling. Green crops are not always practical for landscape situations, but would certainly be effective in new landscapes in the pre-planting phase if time permits.

**Biological inoculants** come as biofertilizers, also called plant growth promoters. They can be in the form of soil bacteria that create symbiotic relationships with legumes, enhancing the nitrogen fixing attributes. Other live microorganisms, such as mycorrhizae fungi, when incorporated into the soil, take up residence around the roots, promoting healthy growth.

Seed from white, crimson, and yellow clover is sown as a green cover crop in April, as soon as the ground can be worked. Clover is hand-turned into soil just before vegetable planting, adding enough nitrogen and organics to the soil to eliminate supplemental fertilizers for the remainder of the season.

**Gypsum** is a mineral that can have some benefits in treating high sodium soils, but it should be applied only when recommended by a soil-testing lab. Lime, also a mineral, is high in calcium and should also only be used per recommendations by an agronomist or extension agent.

**Polymers** are naturally occurring molecules that form long chains made up of thousands of atoms that are bound together in repeating patterns. Chemically produced polymers, when incorporated into soil, increase the length of time the soil holds the water, so they may extend the time between waterings. However, more water must be added to "recharge" the polymers in the soil, so you are not using less water, but you may be applying it less frequently. The amount of water the soil can hold is not increased with the use of polymers. Water-holding capabilities are dependent upon the soil texture, with a fine-textured clay soil holding more water than a sandy, coarse-textured soil.

Polymers cannot affect the evapotranspiration rate, which is directly related to how much water is returned to the soil for good plant health. In the long term, a well-designed irrigation system and careful scheduling are the best water-conserving practices. Polymers used in landscape situations as part of the planting process may prove to be beneficial in maintaining soil moisture for a longer period after transplanting, thereby relieving water stress that might occur post planting.

## COMPACTION AND OVERTILLING

The structure of soil is determined by how the sand, silt, and clay particles fit together to form aggregates. Soil organisms, mycorrhizae, earthworms, and decaying matter are the "glue" that holds the aggregates together. The spaces between the aggregates are the air spaces that provide the pathways for water movement. When the soil is tilled, dug, or moved about, the structure is affected. The aggregates are broken up or compressed (compaction). Excessive tilling or compaction can lead to compromised organic and mycorrhizae colonies and to diminished air spaces. In making improvements to the soil, take into consideration how the solutions affect the soil structure. If turning the soil by hand and shovel to incorporate amendments is unpractical for large landscape areas, then rototill them in, but make minimal passes in order to minimize disruption of the soil and to avoid overtilling or compaction.

## SALINITY IN SOILS

Salts are naturally occurring by a slow weathering of parent material deep within the Earth's crust. Saline conditions also occur from applications of fertilizers and organics, which contain salts. Plant roots have a small amount of salt in their composition, which enables them to create a natural flow of water from the soil to their roots. There is also a degree of salts in the water we use to irrigate.

Soil saline levels are shown to be higher in arid regions. Due to lack of rainfall, there is not enough water percolation into the soil to wash out or leach the salts to a lower soil profile (below plant roots). When air temperatures rise, evaporation from the soil surface is expedited, leaving the salts behind. Poor-draining soils tend to have salt buildup, as the water doesn't drain quickly enough to wash the salts out. Drip irrigation systems apply water slowly and deeply, but the water flow is so slow that salts are not leached out beyond the root zones of the plants.

When salinity levels rise, soil structure is compromised. The high salts separate the soil particles, breaking them apart and creating a tight soil that lacks the air spaces that allow the water to flow through the profile. When salts increase in numbers to more than what the plant produces, the plants cannot absorb the water, leading to water-stressed plants and eventual death.

The first defense is having the soil tested each year for salinity levels and following the recommendations carefully to reduce salts. Recommendations may be as simple as applying

Raised beds solve soil problems. High-saline, slow- or quick-draining, rocky, hard, and lean soils are replaced with nutrient-rich, well-draining, and fluffy imported topsoil mixes.

water to a depth of 10 to 12 inches to leach out salts at the beginning of each growing season. Improve soil drainage with the incorporation of organic amendments to get the water moving. Use of organic mulches reduces evaporation of water from the soil surface, diminishing salt buildup. In extreme saline conditions, the recommendations may require incorporation of specific amendments to break down salts. Importing soils and building raised beds, mounds, or berms may be more costly, but the methods provide long-term solutions for problem soils.

## REDUCE EVAPOTRANSPIRATION

Just as we expel water vapor when we breathe, plants expel water as they transpire. Soil loses water through evaporation. The combination of the two is called evapotranspiration (ET). You can't actually see the process, but put a baggie over a plant and within minutes you will see vapor on the inside of the bag. When a plant is actively growing, it transpires more than its weight in water. A mature oak tree can transpire over 40,000 gallons of water each year.

The ET rate is constantly changing. Rising air temperatures, arid conditions, wind, dry soils, and the age and maturity of a plant are variables that increase the rate of evapotranspiration. The time of year affects the ET rate. Plants tend to slow growth in the winter as the air and soil cool, slowing the rate of water loss. The rate of transpiration is at its peak in mid-spring when plants are actively growing and the temps are still moderate. The ET rate accelerates with the sun rising in the morning and peaks at midday when the day is (usually) at its warmest. The rate decreases as the day wears on, which explains the importance of watering either in the early morning hours or in the evening, when the water has more time to be taken up by the plant and there is less water loss through evaporation and transpiration.

A rational approach to maintaining plant health would be to simply use supplemental watering to replace the water lost through evapotranspiration. This is the goal of irrigation controllers that run on ET rate data collected from nearby weather stations. If only it were that simple. The reality is that most plants get more water than what they need, and the water we do apply is subject to evaporation the minute it leaves the faucet. While we can't control the ET rate, we can minimize water losses through evaporation by applying a layer of mulch.

## ADD MULCH—MANY TYPES

Mulch is a layer of material, organic or non-organic, that is laid upon the surface of the soil, not to be confused with compost, which is incorporated into the soil. Mulch is one of the water conservation solutions that can be practiced immediately, whether the landscape is already established or in planting new spaces. Mulch does double and triple duty in the garden. A layer of mulch:

- protects the soil from wind, air, and sun exposure, minimizing loss of water through evaporation
- shades and cools the soil and plant roots, maintaining soil moisture and slowing transpiration
- captures and slows the flow of water to minimize erosion and water runoff
- creates a dark environment that suppresses weed seed germination
- if organic, decomposes and adds organics to the soil, thereby increasing drainage over time

The mulch you choose depends upon what is readily available, the type of plants you are mulching, your garden style, cost, and labor.

Left: **Mulch is multi-functional in the landscape, conserving water by minimizing evaporation, protecting the soil from erosion, and cooling it down, and by blocking light, it stops weed seed from germinating. Mulch gives the bed a finished, neat appearance, and, applied in a contrasting design, provides an artistic element to the landscape.**
Right: **The mulch display at the Water Conservation Garden, El Cajon, California, exhibits the many organic and inorganic mulch choices available.**

Inorganic mulches are gravel, stone, cinder, sand, and decomposed granite. While they are natural materials, they don't add nutrient value to the soil and should always be used with weed barrier cloth (also an inorganic mulch) laid down before layering on the mulch. The weed barrier cloth allows water to penetrate, eliminates runoff, and provides a layer that keeps the rock, stone, or gravel from infiltrating the soil.

Weed barrier, netting, and woven material do the same job as mulch and are often used on steep slopes before planting to hold in moisture and to minimize erosion. When used in the landscape, they are covered over either with spreading foliage from the plants or from a layer of mulch spread over the top of the fabric.

Organic mulches are shredded bark, wood shavings, tree chippings, pine needles, recycled chipped wood products, and cocoa hulls. Look for uniformly sized particles that are not too small, as they begin decomposing immediately and can be absorbed into the soil, drawing nitrogen in the process. Called "nitrogen tie-up," it can have an adverse effect on the plants in the area. For this reason, fine materials, such as sawdust, are best used for pathways and in small amounts in the compost pile.

If you have large trees that drop their leaves or shed foliage throughout the year, and they are dropping in areas other than lawns, let the leaves remain where they fall. This is a natural mulch and what you typically see when walking through a stand of pine trees or oak trees in their native habitat. If there are other plants in the trees' understories, use a fan rake to knock the leaves onto the ground so they are not shading the foliage. If the leaves fall on the lawn, then save those leaves for mulching other areas or for the compost pile.

Mulch can be purchased in bags or by bulk. Landfills often have clean mulch available at reasonable prices, made from tree trimmings that they have put through a chipper and screen. Arborists and tree trimming companies will sometimes drop a load of beautiful mulch in your driveway for free. I have been spotted chasing down an arborist's truck loaded with mulch and jumping up on the bumper to view it more closely before laying claim. But an easier method would be to make some phone calls to see if they are trimming in your area. Any type of locally grown tree makes for good mulch, except for palms. They don't go through the chipper well and you can end up with large, debris-like shredded pieces that do not make for good quality mulch.

Pine straw mulch is particularly common in the Southeast, where longleaf, loblolly, and slash pines grow natively. There's a trick to spreading this type of mulch without making a mess. Here's how.

1 Buy the mulch. Pine straw is sold in bales, just like hay. Bales can be prickly, and spiders and other insects like to hang out in pine straw, so use gloves when handling the bales. Look for bales that don't appear to have a lot of other material in them—cones, twigs, or pieces of ferns. Pine straw is raked and baled from yards and commercial forests, and sometimes it comes with hitchhiking plants or weeds. Nutsedge is one type of weed that tends to come along, so if you can, put down a pre-emergent herbicide before using pine straw. If you need to control nutsedge that is already sprouting, Image® is the best chemical product to use—it is virtually the only thing that will kill nutsedge.

2 To add the pine straw to the landscape, simply snip the twine holding a bale together, and the bale will break apart into clumps called "flakes." Sprinkle the flakes around the landscape bed or trees, being careful to keep the straw near the ground. If you fling pine straw around above your waist, you'll end up with needles hanging all over your shrubs, and that's annoying to clean up!

3 The newly spread straw will be fluffy, and it will most likely escape the landscape beds. To tidy up the beds, you'll want to rake and tuck the straw to keep it in place. Using a hard rake, pull the straw into the edge of the landscape bed. Step on the straw on top of the rake, and then, leaving your foot where it is, pull the rake out. This bunches up the straw at the edge of the bed.

4 To tuck the straw, after raking, plunge a sharpened spade or shovel into the ground about one inch inside the landscape bed. This will trap the edge of the straw in the soil, and will keep it from blowing out of the bed. You can use a chopping motion to do this.

WATER-CONSERVING SOLUTIONS

Microclimates provided by the berm in the background, large shade trees, and a gazebo make for a cool retreat. The white shrub roses—full sun lovers—appreciate a bit of afternoon shade to cool them down.

Mulch needs to be at least 3 to 4 inches thick to do its job. For new annual plantings or for small plants, apply a 1- or 2-inch layer of mulch, then as the plant grows, add another few inches to complete the process. When applying mulch to trees, leave a 3-inch space around the trunk to avoid rot or molds in times of high rainfall. Replenish organic mulch every three years as it will decompose, leaving soil exposed.

## CREATE MICROCLIMATES

Microclimates, either natural or created, are small areas that reduce evapotranspiration rates *or* speed up the process. The direction of wind, sun, and shade exposure, plant density, expanses of concrete, and soil moisture level all influence microclimates. Use existing microclimates or alter them to accommodate your landscape plan. Create new microclimates to make the most of soil and water resources.

Plants in the shade canopy of a tree or arbor lose only *half* as much water as the same plants in full sun locations. I live in a high desert region, so many full-sun plants are planted under the dappled shade of a juniper, where they flower and thrive in the cooler soil and protected environment. Ivy, garden mums, iris, jasmine, and crape myrtle—typically full sun lovers—appreciate being out of the glaringly hot summer sun in my region.

Planting on the north side of buildings or slopes and under overhangs takes advantage of the microclimates that offer afternoon shade and buffering from the wind. Sun, heat, and—even worse—hot winds can dry out soil and plants quickly. Sometimes the results are irreversible. At my home, we have a long cedar fence lining the property boundaries. The fence forms one side of the vegetable garden, and the shade it produces is valuable gardening real estate. The space has been home to peppers, tomatoes, sweet peas, cilantro, lettuce, and spinach over the years, all of which benefit from the late afternoon respite from the sun.

Above: **An arbor covered with white wisteria blooms and foliage cools down a garden entrance pathway.** Left: **A lettuce bed thrives throughout the heat of summer when planted alongside a fence that provides shade for half of the day.**

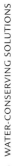

Paved patios, sidewalks, expanses of concrete, and pavers create microclimates that sizzle in the summer heat. Build an overhead, arbor, or trellis along one side to cool things down. Plants living adjacent to shaded hardscapes use half as much water as those right next to them. The reflection of the sun and the heat is very intense in those areas, requiring more water for optimum soil moisture. A thick layer of mulch, a bit of shade cloth, or even planting taller plants to shade the others all help offset the effects of the microclimate.

Match your plant choices to the existing microclimates. If a plant can take a bit of shade, then use the opportunity to increase the green in those areas. Make better use of the permanent structures or hardscapes you have by cooling them with an overhead sail shade, adding some green between any pavers, and mulching around the perimeter. Adding arbors and covered areas provides lovely sitting spaces, but also opens the door to planting spaces and protection from the elements for other plants.

## SHARE THE RESOURCES—HYDROZONING

Developing a water-smart garden landscape will eventually lead to plotting out and locating areas for the plants to grow. Deciding where to put the plants to achieve the look you want is the end design goal. Making water-smart design choices in this planning phase leads to a water-conserving and healthy landscape. Grouping plants with similar water and soil requirements conserves resources as plants share the space, while fulfilling their needs. This practice is called *hydrozoning*.

A lawn has its own water requirements, a shallower root system compared to trees and shrubs, and does best with water applied overhead through a sprinkler, which puts out more water in a short amount of time. Drought-tolerant trees and shrubs, which have deep and far-reaching roots, need water applied directly to the soil, and slowly for a longer period of time in order to penetrate deeply, so drip irrigation is the best method for watering. Some native plants have shallow root systems and don't like to have their "feet" in wet soil, so watering overhead for short amounts of time simulates a summer rain. Each of these situations is accommodated through a system of hydrozoning. The lawn has its own valve and sprinkler system that waters daily, but in short intervals. The trees and shrubs are watered by drip irrigation, on a separate valve or zone, that directs the water slowly to the plant roots for longer durations. The native plantings have an overhead sprinkler system that needs to run just once a week during summer.

Hydrozoning ornamental plants in the landscape is easier for water-smart designs because plant selection is made from a long list of plants classified as drought tolerant. Also, most drought-tolerant plants need well-draining soils, so some of the guesswork is taken out of matching plants with water and soil needs. Water-thirsty plants *can* still be used in a drought-tolerant setting, but they should be relegated to living in a pot where a bit more water can be applied, along with the other container plants that typically need water every day during the heat of summer. Or they can be planted in less arid, more protected, and cooler conditions—for example, in the dappled shade of a tree with other plants that require a moister environment.

One of the first questions an irrigation designer asks is, "What are you planting in this area?" Irrigation systems are designed around your plant choices, but if plants with different needs are growing together, then the plant with higher water needs will suffer from water-stress and the plant that prefers a soil that dries out between waterings will succumb to root rot. When hydrozoning plants in the landscape, consider:

Top, left: **Native plants are interplanted with other drought-tolerant plants from the Mediterranean, South Africa, and Europe. All have similar soil, water, and sun needs, so they can be planted and watered by one zone.**

Bottom, left: **Succulents prefer that their soil dries out a bit between waterings, and they share similar soil and exposure needs—the perfect companions for a separate hydro-zone.**

Right: **A water-thrifty hackberry tree with drought-tolerant fescue lawn planted beneath. The hackberry doesn't mind extra water if planted in a well-draining soil, and the fescue can take a bit of shade, making them good hydrozone companions.**

---

**The plant water needs vary with the plant type.** Most drought-tolerant trees, shrubs, and ground covers share similar amounts of water and the frequency of watering. Succulents, cacti, some native shrubs, ornamental grasses, and wildflowers prefer drying out between waterings (once they are established).

Lawns and meadows should always be on separate valves/zones from trees and shrubs, as they require entirely different watering regimens. If you want to combine the two for a shady or enclosed lawn area, then careful plant selection is vital for the hydrozone to be successful. Some trees and shrubs can tolerate dry or moist conditions; some turf types tolerate shade. Consideration for severe drought or future water rationing might mean sacrificing one or the other. My choice will always be using the water available to maintain the tree, as the turf can always be replaced if it succumbs to drought.

**The deep, wide, or shallow plant roots dictate the amount and method of watering.** Most water-thrifty trees and shrubs have deep-reaching root systems upon maturity, so planting them together and using drip irrigation satisfies all. Groundcover roots spread, so very dense types may compete with other shallow rooting plants for water. However, they would be good choices for slopes, interplanted with deeply rooted trees as they take up different levels of soil space, and one drip system will water all. Some native plants and succulents are shallow rooting, making them good bedfellows, sharing infrequent, short watering cycles with drip or spray irrigation.

Left: **A dwarf citrus tree, in the raised bed in the far corner, shares a hydrozone with the shrub bed that surrounds the lawn, all of which are watered by a drip irrigation system. The lawn is on a separate zone, using overhead spray irrigation.**
Right: **Needlepoint ivy, a full-sun or shade plant, climbs up a native juniper tree. Both are low-water-needs plants and watered on the same zone.**

---

**The exposure preferences of full sun, part sun/shade, full shade, and wind tolerance vary by plant.** Large trees bask in the full sun, but there are smaller tree types that can grow in shady understories of larger trees. In arid, hot-summer regions, some full-sun plants prefer a part sun/ shade setting, making them good companions under trees, shrubs, or in microclimates that give shelter. Full shade, drought-tolerant plants are perfect for planting in dry soils under shade canopies or next to a house in narrow beds shaded by overhangs. Some shrubs can take the heat, but winds may cause their brittle branches to break, so zoning them in a space planted with taller heat lovers gives them the shelter they need.

**The age/maturity of the plant—seedling, juvenile, established, or mature—affects its water needs.** Hydrozoning, in theory, matches water requirements with the plant, but as noted in Chapter 4, water requirements change as plants mature, and different plants mature at different rates. If you are seeding an entire lawn, then adjusting the hydrozone watering to accommodate the needs of the lawn as it germinates, develops roots, and matures is accomplished by changing the run times and duration at the timer. Adjusting the water needs on hydrozoned areas as the plantings mature is done with each successive year they are in the ground.

The challenges come when you incorporate plants at different growth stages into an already planted hydrozoned area. If you plant a drift of wildflowers into the already established meadow, then the newly seeded space will need manual supplemental watering until the seed is germinated and established. Planting young plant starts in a mature landscape requires supplemental watering until they are established. If you are adding trees and shrubs into the established plant zone, then adding a drip line with extra emitters to give them more water their first few years is an easy solution. Any additions, once established, will fit beautifully into the hydrozone area as long as you adhere to the other guidelines listed here.

## INTERPLANTING ORNAMENTALS WITH EDIBLES

Hydrozoning edibles with ornamentals is quickly becoming popular in water-conserving home landscapes. Edible landscapes blend trees, shrubs, vines, and annuals in the landscape so they share resources, while enhancing the space and simultaneously providing homegrown produce. Fruit trees are, with the exception of peaches (which are short lived, just ten years or so), long-living, deep-rooting plants that provide beauty all year. If you live in temperate zones, citrus trees, if mulched, are very heat and drought tolerant and are beautiful landscape trees. Deciduous fruit trees don't require any water during the winter, so irrigation systems are turned off as soon as they are done fruiting and remain off throughout winter until the trees start budding in early spring. They can be quite at home planted as a grove lining the drive, interplanted into a small meadow, pollarded to form a green screen, or used as focal points with shallow rooting herbs, groundcovers, and other ornamentals in their shady understory. Fruit trees fit right into the hydrozone with drought-tolerant trees and shrubs being watered by drip irrigation. If the established fruit tree requires more water during the fruiting stage, then more emitters can be added around its base to supply the extra volume of water.

**A Jonagold apple tree is one of two that flank an entrance drive, beautiful at all times of the year: pinkish-white spring blooms, a shady canopy in summer holding red-blush fruits, golden-yellow to orange fall foliage, and a classic tree silhouette in winter.**

Top, left: **A 'Himrod' grapevine covering a trellis in spring, interplanted with ornamental bulbs at its base.**
Top, right: **'Pink Panda' strawberry is a cultivar produced more for its ornamental value, as it is blanketed in small pink-yellow blooms in spring, but it also produces small edible berries. Its dense growth could cover a slope, while the commonly grown, edible strawberry makes a lush ground cover in landscape beds.**
Bottom: **Greenhouse tomatoes have strong branches and less yellowing of lower foliage than others, making them good landscape companions. Here, they share space with roses; the two plants have similar soil and water requirements. Also in this bed are dianthus, rudbeckia, balloon flower, and seasonal bulbs.**

Berry vines, shrubs, and groundcovers such as blackberry, grape, blueberry, huckleberry, and strawberry can be interplanted into the same hydrozones as ornamentals. Blackberry and grape vines do double duty to cover a fence, arbor, or trellis and they are drought-tolerant plants. Blueberry shrubs have been hybridized to withstand more arid conditions and grow well in the understory of native or other drought-tolerant trees where they receive protection from hot summer sun and winds. Strawberries make a wonderful edible groundcover and could be used on a slope, watered by drip irrigation.

I plant tomatoes in my rose garden every season. Their watering needs are the same during the summer, and the tomatoes are known to be a good pest and blackspot deterrent for the roses. It's also beautiful to see a cluster of tomatoes growing happily and beautifully intertwined with a climbing red rose.

When interplanting edibles with ornamentals, consider the watering needs of the edibles during their juvenile and establishment periods, adding emitters to accommodate the extra water required. Drip irrigation works for all edibles, so incorporating them into existing hydrozones, as long as you pay attention to their exposure needs, provides you with bountiful crops with little changes in the water regimen once the plants are established. All edibles should be mulched and need a well-drained soil, making them good companions for drought-tolerant plants.

## COMPANION GARDENING WITH EDIBLES

I grow all of my family's fruits and vegetables on a little more than an acre of land. Severe water fee increases forced my husband and I to take a hard look at our crops to decide how to continue growing our own food, but to do it on a low water budget. Condensing the crops into one kitchen garden space was the first approach. Widening the planting beds, minimizing pathways, and intercropping vegetable and fruiting crops gave us food for the table and freezer, while our water bill went down. Drip irrigation is run twice daily when the crops are newly planted, then reduced to once a day in early morning by season's end. Straw mulch is used, piled thicker as the crops gain in size. Use the chart below for some compatible garden bed companions and for some that don't care to share bed space.

| Edible | Companionable | Non-Companionable |
|---|---|---|
| Asparagus | Basil, parsley, tomatoes | Potatoes, root crops |
| Beans | Corn, cucumbers, potatoes, radishes, savory, spinach, squash, strawberries | Beets, onion family, sunflowers |
| Broccoli Cabbage family Cauliflower | Aromatic herbs, beets, chamomile, chard, garlic, onion family, potatoes, spinach | Beans, dill, strawberries, tomatoes |
| Carrots | Leek, lettuce, onion family, peas, rosemary, sage, tomatoes | Dill |
| Corn | Beans, cucumbers, potatoes, squash, sunflower | Tomato |
| Cucumber | Corn, beans, nasturtium, radishes, sunflower | Aromatic herbs, potatoes |
| Lettuce | Carrots, radishes, strawberries, tomatoes | None |
| Onion family | Beets, cabbage family, carrots, lettuce | Beans, peas |
| Peas | Carrot, cucumber, corn, beans, radishes | Garlic, onion family |
| Potatoes | Beans, cabbage family, corn | Cucumbers, pumpkin, squash, sunflower |
| Radish | Cucumbers, lettuce, nasturtium, peas | Hyssop |
| Spinach | Lettuce, strawberries | None |
| Squash | Corn, marigold, nasturtium, radishes | Potatoes |
| Tomato | Asparagus, basil, carrots, chamomile, garlic, lettuce, onion family, savory, spinach, strawberries | Cabbage family, corn, fennel |

Left: **The ancient companion planting practice called Three Sisters begins with corn. As the corn grows, bean seeds are sowed at their base, and squash seeds are planted between the rows. The corn supports the beans (nitrogen providers), and squash trails along the ground as a living mulch, shading the sisters' roots.**
Opposite: **Share the water and the soil to have a conserving, productive vegetable garden. Corn shares space with squash; carrots and onions are grown together and harvested at the same time; marigolds deter pests and draw pollinators.**

For many years, I intercropped the vineyard grapes with squash, peppers, cucumbers, and sunflowers. Now that the vines are producing, the water is cut off as soon as they set fruit to avoid splitting, so intercropping plants that require more water in July and August won't work in that location any longer. We plant squash, cucumber, lettuce, spinach, and peppers in the basins of young fruit trees. The roots of the trees are deep, making the sharing of soil space and water possible for annual vegetables.

Annual edibles are considered higher water users than most drought-tolerant crops, so the decision to grow your own depends upon your priorities for your garden space. If it is too much of a strain on your water budget or you lack the space, then container-grown vegetables and fruits are a viable option.

Follow the same water-smart guidelines, check out the list of more water-thrifty edibles in Chapter 8, interplant, and companion plant, and you can have your water-thrifty garden and enjoy a delicious and homegrown harvest, too.

Above: **A retrofit exhibit shows a typical backyard:** a lawn with poor sprinkler coverage leading to browned-out turf areas, shrubs watered by the same system as the turf, and the poor guy pushing a mower, keeping the weed patch lawn in check. Yearly water use: 28,000 gallons!

Left: **The same backyard, retrofitted to water thrifty.** A berm and terrace garden, lush with drought-tolerant shrubs, some hardscape providing a dining patio, cutouts in the fence add light and interest, a small tree for shade, and just enough turf to cool everything down. Yearly water use: 6,000 gallons!

# CHAPTER 6

# Creating a Water-Smart Landscape

e VEN ARMED WITH all the water-smart designs, watering tips, and ways to conserve water, you may wonder where to start. If you are adding a new garden space or starting anew to build a landscape from scratch, begin from the ground up, initiating water-smart methods and water-wise techniques during the planning and construction stages. Grading and contouring lays the foundation for the design and also controls the flow of water. Texture and soil tests, and making adjustments before you plant, help you create a well-draining and healthy soil that drought-tolerant plants need to thrive. Planning the landscape to meet your preferred design style, choosing water-thrifty plants, and matching the irrigation system to the hydrozones create the water-smart garden.

You may already have an established landscape that you enjoy, but you know it is receiving more water than it should. In this case, incorporating water-conserving methods into the existing landscape gives immediate results. Weaning the plants to live on less water, moving some to other beds where they can share water resources, adding mulch to the landscape, conducting an irrigation system check and maintenance, and adjusting the irrigation schedule are actions you can take in your existing landscape to conserve water and enhance plant health.

Or you may have a landscape where some plantings are old, tired, or struggling, but you really love that huge shade tree in the front yard or having a green lawn by the back patio for entertaining. Retrofitting the landscape from water-thirsty to water-thrifty means keeping some of what you like, modifying other areas to be more water efficient, and designing new spaces using water-conserving practices. Creating smaller turf areas, converting high water-use irrigation to an efficient watering system, building the soil, selecting water-thrifty plants and finishing with a layer of mulch completes the retrofit. The old is made new again, the water-smart way.

# How to Be Water-Thrifty Now

First-time homebuyers may be in love with the home they purchased, but have less enthusiasm for the landscape that came with it. Long-time homeowners, with years of time, money, and effort invested in their gardens, may be facing strained water resources, higher monthly water bills, and water rationing schedules that stress the plants that they planted long ago. By adopting even just a few of the water-smart techniques, you'll see immediate water savings and healthier landscapes.

Begin by taking a careful look at your landscape. Walk the garden at different times of the day to see how the sun, wind, or shade affects the various areas. Note the health and vigor of the plants and if they fulfill the role they play in the landscape. Do you rarely sit on the front lawn, but love the huge shade tree that cools the home in the summer? Do the plants along the drive show burned leaves, scant blooms, and little growth? Are there puddles of water in the flowerbed just beneath the rain gutter? What about that rose garden where the weeds grow almost as tall as the bushes? These issues can be addressed using water-smart solutions, and the garden will be healthier with the water-smart changes.

If you initiate just one of the tips below, you can see a 10-percent decrease in the amount of water you use in the landscape and in your water bill. The more water-smart techniques you adopt, the more water-conserving and healthy your landscape will be.

**Keep it clean.** Weeds are defined as any unwanted plants. Weeds give the landscape an untidy appearance, but they also hog water. Weeds send out deep roots and grow quickly, competing for water and soil resources that are needed by the landscape plants. They are also a pest magnet with all their tender, juicy foliage. Once the pests get close enough to your garden plants, they quickly migrate to the really good eats. Pull, dig, or spray out the weeds so desirable plants have access to limited resources.

**Audit water use.** If you have an antiquated irrigation system and it still runs on a regular basis, then obtain a water audit. Contact your local water agency for details. Most likely the service will be free of charge or at minimal cost. Some simple adjustments, revised settings on the irrigation timer, and a parts replacement may be all you need to get dialed into water savings. Drip irrigation systems are easily retrofitted into the existing system, with simple

A typical shrub head riser converted to a drip irrigation system. Conversion fittings are available for retrofitting any spray system to drip or low volume irrigation.

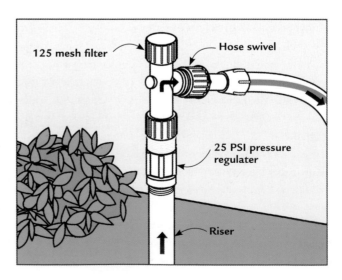

Mulch comes in different sizes, shapes, textures and colors. Select the type based upon the job you want it to do and to match your design style. From top to bottom: white rock; large bark nuggets; color enhanced shredded wood/bark; bulk or landfill mulch; small bark nuggets.

change-outs that you can do yourself. The easiest change is unscrewing the sprinkler head and attaching the appropriate fittings that convert it to a drip line.

**Add mulch.** If all you can do to make your landscape more water-smart is one task, then add mulch. Consult the phone book or local Internet listings for arborists and tree trimmers and start phoning. If you can't track down a company to drop mulch in your driveway, then call the local landfill. Apply a thick layer, 3 to 4 inches, on the surface of the soil. Anywhere you see soil, *even if there is nothing planted in the spot*, apply mulch to minimize water evaporation, hold in moisture, cool the soil, and help control weeds. Mulch can be used on slopes to cut down on erosion, in pathways, on narrow strips along a hot driveway, in play areas, and in open spaces. It is versatile in its use, and the plants where you use it will perk up immediately.

**Minimize or remove turf.** If a lawn is struggling under the shade of a tree, it could be because of the shady microclimate. If the tree is large, the lawn is competing with the tree's enormous root system for water and space. Consider eliminating the lawn and applying mulch. The mulch requires no maintenance, holds in moisture, benefits the tree, and breaks down over time adding valuable nutrients to the soil. If you want to keep a lawn under the tree, investigate shade-tolerant turf types or groundcovers to replace the struggling lawn.

**Install a rain barrel.** Rain barrels are designed to capture the rain that comes off the roof. Even if you only use the rain barrel water for container plants, it is a source of free water and carries some nutrient value with it, too. Look into local and state rebate programs. Some agencies provide a stipend reimbursement to apply toward the cost of the barrel.

**Incorporate organic amendments.** Increasing soil drainage gives roots access to the water; diminishes mucky conditions and standing water in gritty, rapidly draining soils; and increases nutrients in the soil. Spread 3 inches of compost, topsoil, or another organic material of your choice (do not incorporate mulches into the soil; see Chapter 5) on the surface of the area in question, then turn it in with a shovel. You can also lightly hoe it into the surface or work it into the soil with your hands in areas where deep digging might disturb roots. Some root stimulation is not a bad thing, but ripping and tearing of larger roots can send a plant into instant shock. The action of working the soil incorporates the amendments a bit, breaks up any clods and increases airspace. Incorporating organics into bed spaces in preparation for new plantings may eliminate the need of supplemental fertilizers later on.

If you can't put a shovel into the bed due to hard, rocky soil or plant roots, then lay a thin layer of organic amendments on the soil surface, apply mulch, and water overhead once a week during the heat of summer. This process of topdressing is slower, but over the long term, the benefits yield healthier roots and plants.

A green wall made of drought-tolerant and edible grapevine. Fruit and foliage cover the wall from spring through fall, then the drip system is turned off until spring. Golden-yellow to burnt-orange fall foliage comes after, with the twining branches and shredded and gnarled trunks adding winter interest.

**Water the plants.** Trees or shrubs less than five years old need a regular slow, deep soak with a drip system, hose, or soaker hose to encourage their roots to grow deeply. Many problems due to surface roots on older trees that lift driveways and sidewalks could have been avoided with deep watering during their formative years.

Water established plants once every few weeks during the heat of summer, taper off in fall, and water in winter if there is no moisture for one month. Resume watering in spring, but only every two weeks until the landscape is actively sending out new growth. If the landscape is fully mature and it is accustomed to regular watering, then wean the plant to a less frequent watering regimen by spacing out deep waterings over the course of a couple of seasons so the plants can acclimate. (See Chapter 4 for more on watering regimens.)

**Create microclimates.** If that narrow strip along the concrete drive is a hotbed for the struggling plants, then consider planting a row of taller drought-tolerant plants, or install a readymade trellis, fence, or lattice panel to provide shade. Use a soaker hose or drip irrigation to slowly apply water, incorporate compost, add drought-tolerant vines to complete the green screen, and add mulch. You will be amazed at the instant improvement!

# Retrofitting: From Water-Thirsty to Water-Thrifty

As you evaluate your current landscape, the list of challenges to make it more water-thrifty may be extensive. In this situation, it's worth the extra time, effort, and cost to convert a thirsty landscape into a water-thrifty garden. A retrofit allows you to keep established, less-thirsty trees and shrubs, replace others with water-thrifty plants, and incorporate water-conserving practices into the landscape. A retrofit is a way to blend your existing green space with water-smart gardening practices, without having to completely start over in the design/build process.

## RETHINKING TURF AND TURF ALTERNATIVES

In older homes, a green lawn often makes up most of the landscape. Large expanses of turf blanket the landscape, enough to have a good game of sport. A sit-down mower is needed to mow it and cannon-like impact sprinklers water the lawn, along with adjoining sidewalks and driveways.

New home construction places requirements for green space on the part of the builders, so they're not turning over a home with a barren lot to new homebuyers. Sod is an easy, quick, and inexpensive way to add a lot of green to an empty expanse. Typically, a few trees and a lawn fill the space to make up the landscape, with a token three-foot swath of turf running alongside the driveway. There is little thought given to the design or to the efforts and resources required to maintain them.

Personally, I have always been an advocate of turf. I live in a desert, and turf cools the air by degrees, providing a bit of relief from triple-degree summer temperatures. Consider these facts before you eliminate all of your lawn:

- A lawn is made up of millions of individual plants that absorb gaseous pollutants from the atmosphere and exchange that for clean oxygen.
- Lawns trap dust, particulates, and smoke, as well as absorb noise.
- The web of turf roots, which reach deep on low water-use turf types, controls erosion.
- Lawns are a permeable surface and a filter for runoff and ground water contaminates.
- Lawns are fire-retardant, serving as fire-defensible buffers.
- Lawns are 10 to 15 degrees cooler than concrete, asphalt, or other hardscape surfaces.

**Small is better! This 8 x 12-foot fescue lawn is partially shaded by juniper and hackberry trees, mowed tall, deeply watered once a week, and fertilized twice a year, and it provides all the green needed for relaxing, dining, and cooling off on a hot summer day.**

Lawns are still the best choice for play and relaxation, but you only need as much lawn as you can use for these activities. Large expanses are wasteful and use quantities of water, fertilizer, and resources, not to mention the labor involved in maintenance. For example, I have a postage stamp-sized lawn that is used every day during summer, spring, and fall. It is just outside the kitchen door, lending a bit of cool space when the sun heats up that part of the garden quickly in the summer. It measures just 9 feet by 12 feet and can seat up to 12 people dining, with a few dogs thrown into the party.

I water it *entirely* by watering can, dipped into a rain barrel that also captures the water running off the roof from our evaporative cooler in summer. It is not a pristine putting green by any means, but it is green and cool on the feet at the end of the day. I have a friend who uses turf as the paths in her garden. Flanked on both sides by drought-tolerant perennials and shrubs, it is a beautiful green, cool, and soft pathway. It requires just one swipe of the lawnmower and lives happily on the overspray from watering the perennials. There *is* a spot for a bit of green lawn in the water-smart landscape; you just need to limit the size to what you need to do the job.

## CHOOSE TURF TYPES CAREFULLY

Careful selection of the turf type you use is the next consideration. There have been so many developments in hybridizing turf in the last decade that there is a low-water-use lawn out there for every landscape situation. Zoysia and buffalograss, grazing grasses by nature, have been bred for home use. Slow to spread, but very deep rooting, they are low-water-needs grasses that rarely need mowing. Tall fescue, which comes in dwarf types, can take some shade, so planting it under

This turf exhibit shows the many types of water-wise lawns. This photo was taken in the winter months, when some types are dormant or slowed in growth. From left to right: UC Verde Buffalo Grass; Artificial Turf; Blue Rye Mix; Tall Fescue; Hybrid Bermuda; St. Augustine.

your favorite tree makes for a cool, green retreat. Bermudagrass needs some restraints to keep it in bounds, but it is still one of the toughest, most drought-tolerant grasses there is. I have seen it turn completely gray and matted in a summer drought, going into a deep dormant state. As soon as it gets just a bit of water, new green growth appears and fills in like magic.

Turf controls erosion, but you wouldn't plant a type that required regular mowing on a slope. Tall fescue, blue fescue, and other ornamental grasses can be grown on slopes, without any mowing required. For large open expanses and home meadows, deep-rooting blue grama grass offers a drought-tolerant turf solution. Blue grama can be mowed short if you prefer a more manicured lawn, or you can leave it tall and mow it just *twice* on a slope a year, in spring and at summer's end.

There are alternatives to the classic lawn that give green, usable space, but in a new style. Consider planting drought-tolerant groundcovers or perennials en masse on slopes, or water-thrifty shrubs planted in clusters with mulch filling in the spaces in the strip along the driveway. Yarrow, available in many flower colors, can be mowed regularly to encourage spreading; it makes a tough, yet soft underfoot, alternative to a lawn. Creeping thyme, chamomile, and oregano clipped short are sweetly scented alternatives, planted in masses as groundcovers for paths and lawn spaces, planted between pavers, or on slopes.

Wildflowers, bulbs, and ornamental grasses play the part of a lawn, yet only require mowing a couple times a year.

Artificial lawns are alternative groundcovers for shaded areas, poorly drained, boggy soils, or on slopes. They need a bit of ground preparation before installation, so check with the

Meadows planted with turf and ornamental grasses can be mowed shorter (grass on the right) for a conventional lawn or allowed to grow tall (grass on the left), requiring less maintenance and less water. The taller blades shade the root systems and cool the soil, thus retaining moisture longer.

Top: **Creeping 'Pink Chintz' thyme is a low-water-use turf alternative; its delicious scent goes airborne with every step. Creeping thyme makes a water-thrifty groundcover on a slope. Watered by drip irrigation, it can take the heat and only needs a deep, slow watering once or twice a week, with no maintenance required.**

Bottom, left: **A simple, yet attractive, water-wise turf alternative to landscape strips in front of the home, blue grama grass is allowed to grow tall naturally, interplanted with drifts of dianthus that give a spot of color. Both are heat and drought tolerant, requiring just a seasonal maintenance and occasional deep watering.**

Bottom, right: **So many options for ground covers and turf alternatives provide inspiration to creating a lush, xeric landscape in new and exciting ways.**

distributors to see if they offer installation services. They are permeable, allowing the water to percolate into the soil, minimizing runoff. Artificial turf usually comes with an eight- to ten-year warranty, but manufacturers claim that with proper maintenance, the lawn can last up to 25 years. They can be as much as 20 degrees hotter in a full sun location, with reports of artificial turf playing fields being 35 degrees warmer than the air temperature in the summer heat. Artificial turf is an alternative for homeowners who want to eliminate turf as part of the retrofit, but still want the look of a real turf lawn.

The last criterion for selecting lawns or lawn alternatives is to determine how you will water the area. If your lawn area is very small—under 200 square feet—and you are available to hand water, then you can water the area efficiently. For larger areas, especially if you are investing in seed or sod, then a professionally designed irrigation system waters when the lawn needs it, directs the flow, and can be adjusted to accommodate the various growth stages. Avoid irregular angles and incomplete arcs on curvilinear lawns, as these spots are difficult to irrigate. Consider retrofits to the existing irrigation system. Low-flow irrigation heads can be installed into your existing irrigation system. Retrofitting your lawn sprinklers with easy change-outs of conventional spray heads to rotator heads directs the flow efficiently and with less loss of water through runoff or overspray.

Desert areas, locations with severe long-term droughts, and water-challenged communities often have rebate programs in place for homeowners who create smaller lawns or eliminate turf areas and replace them with drought-tolerant plantings.

# Planning and Design

Once the lawn decisions are made, eliminating old and tired plants, heavy water users, or struggling plants will give you a better idea of what areas you have to redesign. Determine the function of the different landscape spaces to plan hardscape features. Overhead structures, trellises, fences, gazebos, and pergolas create microclimates that provide cooling and shading for drought-tolerant plantings. Replace concrete, lifted or unsettled brick pavers, and weed-infested paths with permeable surfaces.

Rainwater catchment systems, contouring, berms and basins, terraces, and drainage should all be considered in the retrofit. Now is the time to address those areas where the water is always running off the planted area and down the driveway. A simple grading and some swales to direct the water coming out of the gutter downspouts to a garden bed directs the flow where it can be used in the landscape. While a total overhaul and grading of your landscape may not be possible, even small adjustments go a long way to conserving water resources.

Drought-tolerant plants (see Chapter 8) should replace the plants that were removed, and then hydrozoned according to their water needs. One of the added benefits of selecting plants with water-saving characteristics is that they usually share nutrient and soil needs, so interplanting is quite easy. If you are integrating new drought-tolerant plantings with established plants, then provide supplemental water to the new plantings

Rain chains slow the flow of rain, directing the drops to the plantings below.

Before: **An expanse of unused turf in a meridian strip, watered more than it needs and with uneven distribution (brown spots on declining turf). The trees provide some shade, growing well in spite of inadequate irrigation. The shade canopies are utilized by the cars parked beneath. Every drop of shade counts.**

After: **This water-wise retrofit, by Steve Harbour Landscapes, kept the trees (now winter dormant), removed the unused stressed turf, and added beach rock mulch, xeric plantings, and installed drip irrigation, creating a beautiful, sustainable, drought- and heat-tolerant landscape.**

until they are established. If the soil is well drained, then the older plants will enjoy the extra bit of water directed at their roots and respond with vigor.

If you find the landscape design process just too daunting to handle yourself, then search for a landscape designer to help you with the retrofit. Landscape designers will assess your landscape and provide a retrofit plan. Then, if you want to do the work yourself, you have a plan of action. The landscape designer will also furnish a list of appropriate drought-tolerant plants for each hydrozone, hardscape suggestions, soil preparation, and irrigation design recommendations.

If you want to plan and design your retrofit, here are a few design basics to get you on your way.

Landscape planning and design are two separate functions. In the planning portion, the plan for the area to be landscaped is put to scale on paper, a preliminary plant list compiled, and special features are designated.

## PLANNING THE WATER-THRIFTY LANDSCAPE

If you have a set of architectural plans with dimensions, it will still be necessary to measure the property lines, noting the exact location of structures, roadways, driveways, existing hardscape features, and utilities. Take precise measurements of the area boundaries, rounding up inches to the nearest foot. Sometimes there is deviation between the architectural drawings and what has actually occurred over time. A few feet can make a big difference.

Locate structures, hardscape features, utilities, or any permanent fixtures on the plan. Be sure to draw in windows, doors, entryways, and overhangs if they will be affected by plant or bed placement. Add existing trees, shrubs, or plants (if they are to remain in the landscape) in the plot plan as if they are at their mature width. Once you have the plot plan drawn to scale, you are ready to start incorporating the list of wants into the spaces.

Take photos and *print* them. Photos tell the true story and give the area dimension and perspective. Show views of the landscape from all angles, including existing structures, adjacent areas, views to enhance, and features to hide.

## ASK YOURSELF THESE QUESTIONS

To develop the planning list, answer these questions:
- · What will the area/garden bed be used for?
- · What sort of foot or vehicle traffic access will be needed?
- · Will the area be visible on all sides? Or just from one?
- · Are there specific objectives for the space? Edibles, ornamentals, bulbs, scented, butterfly or bird garden, lawn for play, entertainment?
- · Are there any limitations? Sewer lines, property lines, power or telephone services, structures, sun or shade challenges?
- · Is there a current irrigation system to retrofit or will you need a new irrigation system?
- · Are there any special design features, favored plant or color palette, water features or hardscape?

## DESIGNING THE WATER-THRIFTY LANDSCAPE

The most important aspect of designing is to follow the horticulturists' creed, "The right plant for the right place." The starting point to achieving this goal is to lay out the space with the mature width/crown size of the plants in mind. By knowing how big the plant is going to

Before: **A water-thirsty landscape, comprised of a struggling lawn, palm trees, and a row of shrubs all on the same watering zone. This family wanted a drought-tolerant, lush retrofit that would save water, require little maintenance, and create a beautiful and inviting entrance to the home.**

After: **The landscape retrofit, by Steve Harbour Landscapes, blends low-water-use flowering shrubs and clumping ornamental grasses, bringing color and flow to the design. A stone wall creates a courtyard. The palm trees and new plantings are watered by drip irrigation, out of sight under the freshly chipped bark mulch.**

**The landscape plan begins with a sketch of the area drawn to scale.**

get at maturity, you'll know how the plants fit the space and how many are needed to fill an area. Allowing the plant to grow into its size naturally creates a healthier plant, the end goal of xeriphitic practices. Designing this way eliminates the necessity of continually trimming every time a branch extends out into the path. With every cut you make, the plant uses more water to generate new growth. Allowing the plant to grow naturally maximizes its drought-tolerant characteristics.

Site the trees on the plan first. They will be the largest and longest living plants in the landscape. Group shrubs and smaller plants in clusters, groups, or drifts of three to five (odd numbers), and build the landscape in layers. Taller plants, growing to 10 to 15 feet high at maturity, make up the background planting. In front of them are the midground plantings, shrubs that reach 5 to 10 feet tall. Smaller plants that grow to 1 to 5 feet tall make up the foreground.

Once you have the space designed, then you have all the information you need to take the plan to an irrigation professional to design a new irrigation system or to help you retrofit the existing system to be more water efficient. For irrigation design purposes, only plant types need to be determined, such as turf, groundcovers, perennials, and shrubs, to plan the best irrigation system to water the zones.

There are rebate programs for landscape and irrigation retrofits, including installing rainwater harvesting storage systems, replacing conventional spray systems with drip irrigation, and using water-smart irrigation controllers. Check with your local water agency for rebate and support programs for retrofitting your thirsty landscape to a water-wise one.

With the plan completed, the excitement builds as all those circles on the plan are given names. It's time to select the drought-tolerant plants.

As the water-smart garden matures, these maintenance tools will be used less, giving more time to enjoy the garden.

# CHAPTER 7

# Maintaining Water-Smart Gardens

**m**OST MAINTENANCE for the water-smart garden begins before planting, while preparing the sites for the plants. This entails breaking ground, working the soil to fluff it up to add air spaces, sometimes incorporating amendments, and monitoring the soil moisture content so the plants begin taking in water as soon as they are planted in the ground. Trees, shrubs, perennials, lawns, and other foundation plants are long-lived, so a few years of maintenance due diligence ensures thriving plants for their 15- to 100-year life spans. The steps we take at plants' beginnings determine how quickly plants recover from transplanting so they can get on with generating new roots and growing.

After planting, plants start sending out tiny root hairs that eventually develop into deep, strong roots. Deep regular watering, maintaining thick protective layers of mulch, selective pruning to encourage strong branch structures, fertilizing (if required), protection from winds and extreme weather, and pest control are ongoing to develop strong healthy structures to acclimate them to the area. Some plants require more care than others, but once established will get on with growing all on their own. The majority of water-thrifty plants, if planted in the right place, don't need pruning, if allowed to grow into their beautiful natural selves. If the soil they are planted in is well draining and they are given all the water they require to establish, they grow deep, healthy root systems to draw in all the nourishment they need from the soil.

When plants are established in the landscape, a gradual reduction in watering over a few seasons will toughen them. There is less pruning as the canopies and natural growth habits take hold. The deep, strong root system is able to draw all the nutrients the plant needs from the soil and transport them through the vascular system to the growing tips of the plant, so there is little need to fertilize. They are prepared to stand on their own.

The trees, shrubs, perennials, and grasses in this home meadow require minimal maintenance now that they are established. Other than trimming sucker growth from the trees, mowing the grama grass meadow, and weed-whacking the phlox once in spring, all that remains is to enjoy the garden.

# Planting and Maintaining the Water-Smart Garden

## PREPARE THE SOIL

Plant in a moist, friable soil. Friable soil is damp enough to make a loosely formed ball in your hands with no water seeping out between your fingers, and the edges of the ball should crumble away easily. Creating a friable soil in the planting hole and in the surrounding area prevents the possibility of adjoining soil wicking away the moisture from the soil in the plant's root zone. Depending upon your soil type, water the area deeply, running the water for short intervals over the course of a couple of days to avoid runoff and to allow the water to percolate deeply into the soil. Then let the soil dry for a few more days until it is friable. I use a soaker hose or drip line for this process, moving it every few hours to another area until the moisture extends 6 to 8 feet out from the planting hole. If the area is to be densely planted, then deeply soak the entire bed.

(See page 67 in Chapter 4 for an explanation of a drip line, emitter, soaker hose, and soaker tape.)

Creating well-draining soils is key to plant growth and long-term health (see more in Chapter 6). Creating airspaces in the soil so water can pass freely is accomplished by turning the soil with a shovel, a rototiller, or with your hands. Working with a friable soil allows you to easily break up large clods and to pull out rocks, weeds, and debris. If you are preparing a new landscape, it's important to work the soil in the entire bed. Chances are it has been compacted

Water the entire area deeply and slowly before planting. This soaker hose ran for a couple of hours just to the point where water began to travel away from the area. The well-draining soil was friable within one day's time, ready to plant.

from the use of equipment and foot traffic, so the entire area needs this initial preparation before digging any planting holes.

Incorporating the backfill (the soil you put back into the hole after planting) with nutrients and compost works well when preparing the soil to plant edible crops or as a seasonal side- or topdressing. However, most drought-tough ornamental plants grow naturally in lean soils; some are legumes, while others are not heavy feeders, so it is best not to amend soils when planting xeric plants. Adding organics to improve drainage may be required, but the entire planting bed should be amended in order to avoid "interfacing," which occurs when a barrier forms where the native soil meets the amended soil. Interfacing can prevent moisture from soaking into the ground, particularly when only the backfill is amended. The new roots eventually will send out growth beyond the amended soil, but sometimes the native soil is so different in texture, it's like a wall stands in the way of root formation. In my garden, I have pulled declining plants out of the ground to analyze and discovered no root growth out of the original rootball even *years* after planting.

## PREPARE THE PLANT

A container-grown plant will show a network of roots when you take it out of the pot, with healthy, white to tan roots, from 1 inch in diameter to tiny, hairlike roots growing to the edges and the bottom of the container. It is not unusual for the roots of larger container-sized plants to wrap themselves in a circle at the bottom of the pot. They have been nursery grown their entire lives, receiving regular fertilizing and watering to keep them healthy and thriving for retail sale. These plants have outgrown the pots, and they need to be either potted into a larger container or planted into the ground.

If there are wrapping or circling roots, then some of the root mass must be removed before planting. If the roots are just loosened before planting, they will continue to circle, eventually girdling (choking) the plant. A 1-gallon plant with circling roots should have the bottom one inch of root mass cut off; a 5-gallon plant, the bottom two inches; a 15-gallon plant should have the bottom 3 inches of circling roots removed. Then, (take a deep breath) using your clippers, slice down the sides of the rootball at three or four places, slicing from top of the root crown to the bottom of the remaining rootball. This slicing should be done on any container plant just before planting; even small 6-pack plants need a clipping from the pruners on each side of their rootball.

The bottom inch of root mass is removed, then the rootball is vertically scored at intervals with a pair of clippers. This eliminates the chance that the roots will circle and girdle the plant and stimulates new root growth.

## REMOVE AND REPOSITION TREE STAKES

A healthy, mature plant needs no staking. It will be able to stand up to winds, to bend slightly with them, to remain anchored in the soil with its deep, wide-reaching roots, allowing the wind to pass through strong, scaffolding branches. Staking is not a permanent fixture. It is a training and supportive tool, used while the plant is becoming established, then removed so the plant can stand on its own. Container-grown trees usually come with a stake or two that are tightly tied to the tree in a few spots up and down the trunk. If the stakes are left in place, then the cell tissues alongside the stake will not receive light, causing them to elongate, leading to a weak trunk. Eventually the tree's crown will flop over or snap, because it does not have a strong supporting cell network.

When you bring a tree home, remove all stakes and ties before planting. Re-stake only if the tree is unable to stand on its own or if high winds are typical where you live. Add the stakes after planting, evenly placed at least 4 inches away from the trunk, and tied loose enough to allow the tree to move with the wind, but tight enough to keep it from rocking in the soil. Space the stakes farther away from the trunk each year, with the aim of removing them by the time the tree has been in the ground for three years.

## PLANT

Dig the hole just as deep as the depth of the rootball and twice as wide. Bare-root plants need to sit upon a mound of soil in the hole that is high enough for the soil level to be exactly the same as it was when planted in the ground. Seedlings; annuals; 4-, 6-, and 8-inch; quart-sized; and flats of rooted cuttings require the same attention to planting depth, but are often planted in large quantities in the same bed. Dig the entire area to the depth needed, arrange the plants as you need them, then backfill the entire bed, bringing the soil to the same level as they were in the containers.

Deep planting—burying the trunk above the point where it was originally growing, whether in the ground, in a container, or field dug (balled and burlapped)—will be detrimental to the plant. Seedlings that are deep planted can succumb to stem rotting overnight; young starter

Left: **Note the large berm and basin on this just-planted ash tree. It will be enlarged each season to accommodate the growing rootball and canopy. The sapling will require a basin full of water every three to five days for the first month to get it through initial transplant shock.**
Right: **A properly staked tree allows for some movement so the tree can sway with the breeze. These stakes should be spaced farther away from the trunk each year, until the tree's own scaffolding supports the tree, at which time (three to five years) the stakes should be removed.**

plants will rot in a week's time; shrubs and perennials drop their leaves and collapse in a matter of months; trees may take a couple of seasons to show the effects of deep planting. The trunk or stem slowly rots, leading to a yellowing of leaves on old and new growth that eventually turn crispy brown. The plant defoliates, the rotted base causes a collapse of its root system (restricting its vascular system), and the tree fails. All this occurs long after you thought the tree was on its way to establishment. Deep planting occurs at planting time with piling the soil high on the trunk, and it also occurs post planting, if the tree settles in the hole and the soil walls cave in to cover the root crown.

Here's the right way to plant: set the plant in the hole, adjust the height so it sits a bit higher than it was before (to account for settling), then backfill, tamping the soil around the rootball so the soil is firmly placed against the roots. Work the backfill soil with your hands or shovel to further fluff it up and create airspaces before you put it back in the hole. Continue to tamp the soil as you fill the hole, but don't press too firmly or you will eliminate all the airspace you created, compacting the soil. When the soil is at the level you want it, build a broad berm

1 Use a shovel or marking paint to mark the area for the hole. The planting hole should be twice as wide as the tree's rootball.

2 Dig the planting hole. This hole should be just as deep as the rootball—no deeper! If you sharpen the spade before digging, this step will go faster.

3 Set the tree in the planting hole to check the depth. If the top of the rootball is lower than the soil line around the edge of the planting hole, add some soil back into the hole, pull the tree out of the pot, and replace the tree in the hole. You never want the crown of the tree (where the tree trunk meets the tree roots) to be below the soil line.

4 Fill in around the tree with the same soil that you removed from the planting hole. Do not add fertilizer or new topsoil. Water will move more easily and the tree will root properly if the soil in the planting hole and around the planting hole are the same.

around the plant, creating a basin that encompasses the entire rootball and extends beyond the farmost branches. When completed, the basin should be at least three times the diameter of the rootball. (For more, see tree berm and basin, Chapter 3.) If you are planting entire beds at a time with smaller plants, then there is no need to build berms.

## WATER THE PLANT

Fill the basin slowly with water, allow it to drain, and then refill it a number of times to ensure that the water has penetrated beyond the rootzone. Use a hose set to a trickle, a soaker hose, or a drip line to water-in bed plantings, allowing the water to penetrate slowly and deeply throughout the bed. Maintain this moisture level for a couple of weeks, then gradually taper off watering to a couple times a week during the plant's first summer. (For post-planting watering guidelines, see Chapter 4.)

Install drip irrigation tubing *before* adding mulch. Avoid piling mulch directly against the trunks of trees and shrubs; leave a 3- to 4-inch mulch-free zone around the base of the plant. Extend the mulch area to cover the area outside the basin. Spread a few inches of mulch in the entire bed area when planting small plants, adding mulch as the plants grow.

---

**This soaker hose provides water to the entire tree root zone. Wind the hose around the base and extend it beyond the drip line of the tree, where mature roots grow. Allow the soaker hose to run for a few hours until the soil is deeply watered.**

Think before you cut. Allow plants to grow into their natural form. If you have to prune to shape, do the task in early spring before bloom begins.

# Maintaining the Water-Smart Garden

## A BIT ABOUT PRUNING

Back away from the pruners! As you read about water-thrifty plants, you may notice there is not much about pruning. If the right plant is in the right place, then it's best to let it grow naturally, only trimming errant branches on shrubs, ground covers, and perennials.

Trees should not be pruned until they have been in the ground for three years. The pruning rule of thumb can be summarized as the "Three Ds": prune only dead, damaged, or diseased branches. Other pruning basics to consider:

- Think before you cut. Every cut you make affects the growth and health of the tree—forever. If you are unsure, then don't cut.
- When trees are young, trim crossing branches if they are obstructing the growth of other branches or growing inward.
- Never make cuts beyond the branch collar.
- Suckers, growth that sprouts from the trunk, and water sprouts, weak upright growth coming from the branches of the tree, should be removed as they are weak and unsafe.
- Trees should never be topped.
- Fruit trees should be pruned according to species guidelines.
- Pruning large, mature trees should only be done by a certified arborist.

## A BIT ABOUT NUTRIENTS

Most drought-tolerant plants are not heavy feeders. They live naturally in lean, arid soils. Key to their success is providing a well-drained soil so that the roots can absorb water and nutrients from the soil. The basic nutrients that plants need—nitrogen, phosphorus, potassium, iron, calcium, manganese, and zinc—are present in native soils. Trees, shrubs, perennials, succulents, and groundcovers thrive on what nature provides. Adding fertilizer just encourages faster and more growth. Incorporating a timed-release fertilizer can help a plant recover from transplant shock and speed growth, but deep watering and a well-drained soil get the same results. Bulbs, small storage vessels themselves, get off to a good start with a formulated, balanced bulb fertilizer. Some turf types respond to fertilizers by greening up quicker after winter dormancy, producing more leaf blades and greener, lusher growth. Native plants and those that come from arid regions can show toxicity to added nutrients with burned leaf tips, with damage extending throughout the plant. If a plant slows growth, stops producing foliage, or shows changes in leaf color, then check the moisture content in the soil first, as symptoms for water stress and nutrient deficiencies are similar. If the soil is evenly moist, take a soil sample to a nursery professional or to the cooperative Extension for diagnosis and recommendations before you fertilize.

## A BIT ABOUT PESTS

If a plant is healthy, it can win the battle against pests. Pests usually have favored spots to graze first. New foliage is tender and chewy, and appeals to caterpillars horned worms. The undersides of leaves are easy access to the veins for sucking insects like aphids. Others prefer the stems (scale) and where the branches meet the stems (mealybugs). Tomato horned worms, which eat pepper plants, too, can be handpicked when they are foraging, in early morning or at dusk. Aphids, mealybugs, and scale can be controlled by a hard blast of water and by handpicking.

Spider mites and leaf miners, not visible to your eye except by their finely spun webs or burrowing patterns in the leaves, can diminish by repeated hard blasts of water. If that fails, you may need to resort to an organic control or repeated releases of beneficial insects. If you do use chemical controls on rampant pests in the landscape, that should be done in the early morning hours when there is no wind, and always follow label directions.

Beneficial insects that prey upon the pests usually hatch later in the season, which is nature's way of making sure there is an ample food source for them. Sometimes a bit of patience and nature takes care of the pests. If large trees are showing heavy infestations of aphids and raining a sticky residue, then repeated releases of ladybugs or praying mantis can bring the populations

Tomato horned worms chew tomatoes and peppers. They forage in the early morning and evening, so hunt for them then. They are camouflaged in the foliage and stems, but their presence is made known by the stripped and chewed leaves. Look just below the ravaged spots to find them.

As soon as you see fruit and a population of birds hanging about waiting, then net. We run the netting over the entire row of grape vines, draping it down to the ground and closing the bottom with clothespins. Otherwise, the birds will find entry and eat the entire crop overnight.

under control. If you need immediate controls, hire a licensed pest control operator to do the job properly and safely.

Of bigger issue (for us) are the pests that threaten our food crops. The sustainable approach is to keep the plants healthy, intercrop with other plants that are pest deterrents, practice crop diversity, and tolerate a bit of damage to the crop. Birds, squirrels, and chipmunks can ravage an entire tree or vine overnight. Netting to encompass the entire plant is our only control. Ground dwellers such as moles and gophers are killed in traps.

## LET THE PLANTS DECIDE

If a plant doesn't seem happy after a few seasons of being in its new home, then consider moving it to another location. Maybe the browning leaf tips of the succulents are getting too much summer sun. Move them under the dappled shade of the hackberry, and they will sit up and take notice. The crape myrtle struggles to leaf out every year in its protected location away from the wind. Moved it to a sunnier spot, still gaining wind protection from a nearby purple leaf plum, add a few more inches of fresh mulch, and it will thrive. I tried repeatedly (with many plants) and without success to coax variegated ivy to trail over the rock wall. The poor things barely sent out any foliage at all no matter how much water I gave them. I finally moved them under the shade of the native juniper, where they are climbing happily to the top. I learned that nothing wanted to live on that hot, blazing-in-sun spot. Now it is blanketed with fresh shredded bark every season, a lovely no-care groundcover.

As plants mature, they become more self-sustaining, strong enough to take whatever Mother Nature sends their way. Water-thrifty gardens are meant to be enjoyed. If they are happy in their environment and established, you can put the tools away, have a cool drink, and just sit and enjoy the view. Water-thrifty, water-wise, water-conserving, the water-smart garden demands your attentions in its beginning, but then gives back to you, your children, and their children for years to come—all on its own.

Even heat- and drought-tough succulents may need a break from triple-digit temps in summer. These perked up immediately once they were moved under the dappled shade of a juniper tree. Watch the plants for signs showing that they are unhappy in their situation, then accommodate them.

# Water-Thrifty Plants

t HE MOST DIFFICULT PART of listing water-thrifty plants is that there are *so many* of them that it seemed impossible to hone out favorites to fit into this short chapter. There are drought-tolerant plants that grow naturally across the U.S. in *every* region and climate. They grow in colonies and drifts, sustaining themselves on nothing more than what nature provides, and have perpetuated their species through hundreds of years of extreme weather conditions. Plants that live in arid, dry regions from all over the world make their way to our gardens, growing naturally in rocky scrub, prairies, woodlands, dry streambeds, and hillsides, thriving in our climates and soils, too.

Knowing *where* a plant grows naturally gives clues to the environment it needs to thrive. Most drought-tolerant plants are not picky about the soil. If they grow naturally in arid areas, thriving in alkaline, lean, and dry soils, then soil prep is an easy task—no amendments or supplemental fertilizing necessary. Rocky, dry, and sloping native habitats tell us that the plants live in well-draining sites and are not slowed by lean, gritty, rocky, and low-nutrient conditions. Some drought-tolerant plants live in dry, open scrub, but also thrive at the edges of woodlands, which means they can be grown in a landscape that is allowed to dry out between waterings *or* they can grow in an area that receives regular watering.

---

**Select water-thrifty native plants and combine them with plants from around the world that thrive in arid climates to create a beautiful, textural, all-seasons interest water-smart garden.**

Left: **Pinyon pine is native to high desert and mountain elevations throughout the southwest. Growing naturally in rocky, lean soils; arid climates; and where high winds blow year round, it is a good choice for open, sunny sites in USDA Zones 5 to 8, and is tolerant of any soil, if well-draining.**
Right: **Mexican hat,** *Ratibida columnifera*, **native to the central plains and western states, reseeds freely in the home landscape, but is not classified as invasive. Buy the seed or starts from the garden center and allow Mexican hat to naturalize in your garden.**

# What Makes a Plant Drought Tolerant?

All plants lose leaves if they are summer- or winter-dormant, and evergreens continuously shed older foliage. In their native habitats, leaves stay where they fall, creating nature's mulch. Succulents and other desert dwellers use the sand, gravel, or stone as mulch. Woodlands, meadows, and forests have leaves, needles, pine cones, and bark shavings (such as that of junipers, which shed their bark) at their feet, mulch that comes their way naturally. Recommended mulches in each plant profile are based on the type of mulch they'd receive in nature. Succulents, some grasses, and native species prefer rock, sand, or gravel mulch. Chipped or shredded bark works better for plants originating from woodlands, forests, or open meadowlands.

Plants that are native to the U.S. have proven their ability to live on what Mother Nature provides, so if we can mimic their native habitats as closely as possible, then success is assured. They have the ability to survive and multiply in the outback, proving that they tolerate drought, wind, and weather extremes, all characteristics that make them workhorses (once established) in our gardens. A caution: By moving them to our landscapes, though, we take them out of nature where their populations and maximum growth have been restricted by competing species, rainfall, weather patterns, grazing, and foraging animals. Plant them in our gardens, give them many more resources than they have in nature, and they *can* threaten other species by colonizing or even becoming invasive. Garden centers that sell native plants are aware of species that carry the threat of being invasive, so they will note that on the plant label, and plant breeders provide us with less invasive options through cultivars. Make native plant selections carefully, read their labels, and only buy from reputable growers or nurseries. Never dig plants out of the wild and transport them home.

Look for xeric leaf characteristics—needle-like, narrow, linear, serrated, deeply lobed, finely divided, rough, hairy, smooth, waxy, oily, gray- or blue-green, white, silver, or variegated foliage—all features that contribute to plants being plants drought-tough, once established.

## CHARACTERISTICS OF DROUGHT-TOLERANT PLANTS

One characteristic most drought-tolerant plants share is that they have deep, far-reaching root systems that give them access to moisture in the soil. Drought-tolerant plants need deep, infrequent water until they are established, then supplemental water if there are short droughts during summer.

Water-thrifty plants have leaf characteristics that help them conserve moisture. Succulents and cacti store water in fleshy leaves, giving them the ability to use water reserves as they need them. As you examine these plant lists, note that water-saving characteristics are italicized. The more familiar you become with these special characteristics, the more able you will be able to pick other xeric plants out of the crowd. Even if the label doesn't give you insight as to their drought tolerance, the plants will. Look for the following characteristics:

**The size of the leaf.** The larger the leaf, the more water a plant needs to thrive. *Small, needlelike, linear,* and *narrow-leaved* plants need less water to grow. They grow in abundance up and down the stems of drought-tolerant plants and offer protection from scorching sun and wind, each small leaf conserving a tiny bit of moisture.

**The leaf margin.** *Serrated* or *toothed* leaf margins (the outer edge of the leaf) break up the flow of water as it comes off a leaf surface, trapping moisture in its jagged cuts. *Finely divided, feathery, deeply lobed, curled,* or *ruffled* edges are moisture-saving characteristics.

**The leaf surface and color.** *Rough, fuzzy, hairy,* and *deeply veined* leaves capture water on the leaf; *shiny* and *waxy* leaf surfaces and leaves that contain *oils (scented)* offer protection for the leaves from drying out and from sunscald. *White, silver,* and *gray-* or *blue-green* leaf colors are common in desert xeric plants, to better reflect the harsh sunrays. Leaves with *deep green topsides* and *white or lighter undersides* or *variegated* with white or lighter stripes also reflect the sun.

## WHEN TO WATER

The seasons during which plants are actively growing determine when we can eliminate or reduce watering. Deciduous plants don't need water during their dormant periods; evergreens slow their growth in cooler weather so they require less water during that time. General watering tips are listed in each plant profile. Good watering practices while the plants are immature lead to healthy, strong, drought-tough mature plants (for more, see Chapter 4).

## KNOW YOUR ZONE

Each plant, except for annuals, is listed with the USDA zones in which it thrives. Learn the zone you live in (see USDA Zone Map, page 10) if you don't already know it, and trust your local garden centers to stock the plants that grow successfully in your zone. (The nursery trade markets and sells annuals that *do* have short lives in the heat. However, nurseries want to sell trees, shrubs, and longer-living plants that can grow in their area. The goal is to make a buyer successful so he or she comes back and buys more. If they offer a plant that is marginal in their respective area, they'll list that information on the label. Proper labeling is required by the American Nursery Association.)

The zone range listed in the plant profiles encompasses the entire genus. Individual species and cultivars that are successful in your area are the plants offered for sale. Read the labels and be prepared to venture out of your comfort zone to try new plants. Sometimes providing the right microclimate, adding a thicker layer of mulch in winter, or giving more shade in summer can help a plant establish and adapt to its environment.

## GROW FROM SEED

Annuals, edible annuals, garden-sown perennials, and some turf species can be grown easily from seed without the need for a greenhouse or propagation facilities. Propagating from seed expands the options of species, colors, sizes, and growth habits, creating a dizzying array of choices. It takes a watchful eye, though, providing the right soil, exposure, seedbed preparation, and constant moisture while they are germinating, but after you've experienced the rush of growing from seed, the possibilities are endless.

Left: **Agastache, or hummingbird mint, can be propagated from seed. After four sets of leaves form on the tiny seedlings, they are transplanted into 2-inch pots. When roots have filled the pots and after the last frost, the plants are placed in the landscape.**
Center: **Pull the plant out of the pot and look at the roots: they tell the story of the health of the plant. These roots are white to tan, no bigger than a pencil, and reach to the bottom of the pot, all signs of a healthy, growing plant.**
Right: **This currant, clove-scented ribes, was planted from a quart-sized pot. Eight years later, it is mature and well established, surviving and thriving on natural rainfall and with no supplemental fertilizer or maintenance.**

A beautiful, lush, water-smart landscape began as 4-inch to 1-gallon sized plants. Now, the garden thrives in maturity.

Container-grown perennials, groundcovers, ornamental grasses, shrubs, and trees are worth the investment. They have well-established root systems, you can visualize how they will look in the landscape, and you can determine flower and leaf colors before you buy. The smaller the plant you put into the ground, the longer it takes a plant to grow to maturity. Most low-water-use plants are slower growers by nature. However, the longer the plant is in the ground, the stronger and more acclimated it is (so installing smaller plants is actually better). If you want instant gratification, then buy larger containers, but be prepared to give them all the water and attention they need to plant them in their new home (see Chapter 7).

# Time to Shop

When you shop, feel free to pull the plant out of its pot and check the roots. I consider it the equivalent of squeezing a melon at the market. The health of a plant's roots determines the health of the plant. What you want to see is firm white or tan roots that grow to the bottom of the container. The soil should smell fresh. If there are dark brown or black soft, mushy roots and a foul smell, it's probably a sign of root rot: best to move on to another plant. Rootbound plants have roots that are wrapping around themselves, a condition that is not detrimental if extra pre-planting procedures are followed (see more in Chapter 7).

The plants described in the following list are just a sample of what is available in seeds, plants, or starts. Begin your design with trees to set the foundation to your landscape. Add some shrubs to define an area, bulbs and annuals for punches of color, and reliable perennials for accents. Cover an arbor, blanket the ground, or dig your toes in a cool lawn. Fill the hot spots with succulents and ornamental grasses, and interplant open spaces in the landscape with edibles. Capture your style, set the mood, and create an oasis the water-smart way. The water-thrifty possibilities are endless!

# African Daisy

*Dimorphotheca sinuata*

African daisy, native to southern Africa, basks in summer heat and full sun, covered in daisylike 1½- to 2-inch white, pink, orange, and purple blooms held above deep green, *slightly serrated foliage*, from early spring through summer until first frost. **SIZE (H × W):** Mounding 6 to 12 inches x 12 inches. **SUN:** Full sun; blooms close at night and only partially open on cloudy days. **MULCH:** Natural wood chips or shredded bark. **LANDSCAPE USE:** Plant in sweeps throughout the garden to accent focal point shrubs. Planted en masse, it makes a carpet of color around trees or on a slope. Interplant with full-sun plants and grasses in containers and in perennial gardens or along meadow edges as a filler. New cultivars available in early spring in seed, 6-packs, 4-inch, and quart-sized pots. Water deeply, infrequently through summer.

# California Poppy

*Eschscholzia californica*

When the Anza Borrego Desert receives winter rains, California poppies quickly germinate in early spring. *Finely divided, gray-green, feathery foliage* forms, followed by delicate 8- to 24-inch stems holding bright orange flowers that cover the desert floor. Replicate poppy fields by broadcasting seed in early spring in cold-winter areas for summer blooms; sow in fall for spring flowers in warmer winter climes. Gently tamp seed in, cover lightly with sand. **SIZE (H × W):** 12 inches x 18 inches. **SUN:** Full sun. **MULCH:** Sand, beach stone, or bark mulch applied when plants are 6 in. tall. **LANDSCAPE USE:** Plant in drifts in home meadows, on slopes and hillsides, or between shrub groupings. Seed and packs available in orange, red, white, yellow, pink, and rose. Keep seedbed moist until germination; reduce watering until you see signs of wilt, then sprinkle lightly.

# Cosmos

*Cosmos bipinnatus*

Cosmos grow naturally in meadows in the southern U.S. in full, hot sun and like well-drained soil. Cosmos self-sow *everywhere*, even popping up in gravel driveways—testament to their toughness and versatility. *Finely divided, feathery foliage* covers tall, strong, woody stems that send out white, purple, pink, red, and lavender ray flowers in early summer, continuing through first frost. **SIZE (H × W):** To 3 to 4 feet x 1½ x 2 feet. **SUN:** Full sun. **MULCH:** Gravel, natural wood shavings and chips in the landscape, straw in vegetable gardens. **LANDSCAPE USE:** Interplant with edibles, in drifts as midground plants in cut-flower gardens, broadcast seed at meadow edges, en masse in perennial beds, and in containers. Pollinator magnets, cosmos tolerate moist or dry conditions. Fast growers from seed or packs. Water deeply, infrequently through summer.

# Gazania

*Gazania hybrids*

Gazania has broad distribution, growing in desert elevations and coastal regions of South Africa. The foliage is *gray to white on the undersides with a fuzzy coating*. There are clumping and trailing species in yellow, orange, white, pink, red, burgundy, and multicolored hybrids, blooming from early spring through summer. **SIZE (H × W):** Clumping to 8 x 10 inches; trailing types 8 inch x 24-inch-long stems. **SUN:** Full-sun annual and perennial (in temperate climes). **MULCH:** River rock, shredded or chipped bark. **LANDSCAPE USE:** Plant singly in rock gardens, in masses as a border, in drifts interplanted with shrubs, and in containers. Colorful accent to conifers, succulents, agave, and sedum, and as a foil for bulbs. Trailing types are excellent erosion control for slopes in temperate climates. Hybrids in seed, packs, quarts, 1-gallon pots, and flats. Water deeply, infrequently.

# Globe Amaranth

*Gomphrena globosa*

Globe amaranth heralds from the deserts of Australia and tropics of South America. Tough, heat-loving, open-branched plants with stiff stems are covered with *lancelike leaves*. Tall, 12-inch stems hold white, purple, red, or orange globe-shaped blooms with contrasting bracts from summer to fall. **SIZE (H × W):** 12 to 24 inches x 12 inches. **SUN:** Full sun or part sun/shade. **MULCH:** Shredded or chipped bark mulch. **LANDSCAPE USE:** Plant globe amaranth closely in a pot, group together for a border planting, or plant en masse in a cutting cottage garden. Plant in dappled shade in the understory of open-branching trees; plant white-flowering types in sweeps to emphasize bushy green shrubs and for a night garden. Buy bud-tight packs in early spring. Cut flowers to dry for winter use. Water deeply, infrequently, and avoid wetting foliage.

# Lantana

*Lantana* spp.

Lantana grow naturally in tropical regions of South Africa, and North, South, and Central America. A heat-loving perennial in warm, frost-free areas; long-blooming, quick-growing annual elsewhere. *Roughly textured foliage* with spring to fall blooms, mimicking tiny bridal bouquets, in combinations of bright white, orange, red, purple, pastel pink, lavender, and yellow. **SIZE (H × W):** *L. camara*: 1 to 3 feet x 1 to 4 feet; *L. montevidensis*: 2 feet x 6 feet. **SUN:** Full sun. **MULCH:** Chipped bark. **LANDSCAPE USE:** Long-lasting color and groundcover. Plant singly, allowing plants to trail over the edges of pots, mix with upright, linear foliage plants for contrast. Use as filler in perennial gardens or in color borders. Plant in masses on slopes for erosion control. Available in 1-gallon pots in early spring after last frost. Water deeply, infrequently; avoid watering leaves.

# Marigold

*Tagetes* spp.

Marigolds grow naturally on hot, dry slopes of Mexico and open valleys in South America. *Aromatic, deeply divided* and *serrated leaves*; double or single flowers in one or a combination of colors including bright yellow, orange, burgundy, and creamy yellow. **SIZE (H × W):** All sizes from 4 inches x 12-inches to wide-branching 4 feet x 2 feet. **SUN:** Full sun. **MULCH:** Wood chips. **LANDSCAPE USE:** Plant taller types in cut-flower gardens, smaller branching marigolds in drifts in the foreground, and French types en masse in color borders. Interplant edible-flowered plants in vegetable gardens as natural pest deterrents and as colorful tasty companions. Self-sowers; easy to grow from seed. Plant packs and pots in fall for spring blooms in desert climes; in spring for summer to first frost blooms in colder regions. Water infrequently and deeply.

# Mexican Hat

*Ratibida columnifera*

Mexican hat are native to the western and central prairies of the U.S., colonizing in Mexico and Canada. Heat-loving annual to biennial plants, with clumps of *deeply cut leaves* that lay close to the ground. *Hairy, narrow stems* rise above the foliage, holding a dark cone "hat" with yellow or maroon/yellow petals forming the brim. From early spring to fall, the blooms make long-lasting cut flowers; dry the cones for later use. **SIZE (H × W):** 24 inches x 18 inches. **SUN:** Full sun. **MULCH:** Stone, sand, river rock. **LANDSCAPE USE:** Prairie gardens, meadow plantings, in drifts in the cut-flower bed, tucked among boulders in rock gardens, or en masse along dry streambed edges. Sow from seed in spring or buy in pots and allow to reseed. After establishing, allow soil to dry before watering.

# Moss Rose

*Portulaca grandiflora*

Moss rose grows naturally in South America in dry, sandy soils while basking in heat. *Fleshy, succulent, cylindrical, pointed leaves* grow on bright red trailing stems that stay low to the ground in mosslike fashion. Rose-shaped, single or double, 1-inch flowers open in sun in bright hues of red, orange, yellow, white, and bicolors on a single plant, or buy seed or plants of one color. **SIZE (H × W):** 6 inches x 18 inches. **SUN:** Full sun. **MULCH:** Stone, river rock, sand, bark chips. **LANDSCAPE USE:** Hanging baskets, mounding between stones in rock gardens, trailing along the ground in succulent beds, and spaces in the front of color borders. Available in early spring as seed, packs, or in pots for spring through fall blooming. Infrequent watering.

# Poppy

*Papaver* spp.

Poppies grow naturally as annuals (sometimes biennials or perennials) in a wide range of climates in central and southern Europe, Asia, and Australia. *Finely divided, toothed, fuzzy, or hairy leaves* range from *deep- to gray-green*. Stems rise above clusters of foliage and *may be covered in fine hairs*, blooming orange, white, red, yellow, salmon, pink, rose, purple, and combinations. **SIZE (H × W):** 18 to 36 inches x spreading 6 to 12 inches. **SUN:** Full sun. **MULCH:** Sand, gravel, stone, wood chips. **LANDSCAPE USE:** In areas with cold winters, broadcast seed in fall for early spring blooms in sweeps in open beds, along meadow edges, scattered over the tops of bulb beds. In temperate areas, sow in late winter to early spring for summer blooms. Available as seed, packs, and pots in early spring. Only lightly water overhead when bloom starts.

# Pot Marigold

*Calendula officinalis*

Calendula grow naturally in rocky, arid, hot, full sun to part-shade locations from southern Europe and northern Africa. Pot marigold has an open-branching habit, its stems lined with *lancelike, sticky, aromatic foliage*. Single or double blooms in a riot of colors in orange, yellow, cream, apricot, pink blush, and with red or burgundy accents. **SIZE (H × W):** 12 to 30 inches x 12 to 18 inches. **SUN:** Full sun. **MULCH:** Wood chips, river rock. **LANDSCAPE USE:** Grow clumps in containers, in drifts planted in color borders, in sweeps at meadow edges, in cutting garden foregrounds, and in edible gardens as a colorful, spicy salad ingredient. Leave some blooms to self-sow the following season. Sow from seed in spring after last frost in cold regions, in fall in desert climates; packs and pots available. Water deeply, infrequently.

# Tidytips

*Layia platyglossa*

Tidytips are native to the western U.S., growing in meadows and grasslands in lean sandy or rocky soils. Tidytips form mounds with their *gray-green, fuzzy, narrow, toothed- or smooth-edged leaves*. They begin flowering in early spring with bright yellow, daisylike flowers blanketing the plant. **SIZE (H × W):** 18 inches tall and wide. **SUN:** Full sun. **MULCH:** Sand, rock, gravel, wood chips. **LANDSCAPE USE:** Use tidytips wherever you need a bright color boost, in front of garden borders, interplanted in sweeps in perennial gardens, in clumps in rock gardens, interplanted with ornamental grasses in meadows, and in containers. In temperate climates, tidytips will self-sow and naturalize. Sow seed in fall for early spring bloom (if in a mild winter area); otherwise sow seed in early spring or buy starts in packs. Allow soil to dry before watering deeply.

# Crocus

*Crocus* spp.

**ZONES:** 3–9. Crocus grow naturally in dry, arid scrublands, meadows, and woodlands in the Mediterranean, Middle East, Africa, and China. Crocus bloom in autumn, winter, and early spring, depending on the species. They have *linear grasslike leaves* and cup-shaped flowers in yellow, pink, purple, peach, and lavender, with some streaked in contrasting colors. Some are sweetly scented and some are edible (saffron crocus). **SIZE (H × W):** Flower stems 2 to 4 inches x spreading. **SUN:** Full sun, or part shade in hotter summer climates. **MULCH:** Shredded bark. **LANDSCAPE USE:** Plant in clumps for a good show, sited near paths and seating areas to catch the scent. They make good container plants. Use singly in rock gardens, in sweeps in color borders, bulb beds, and meadows. Plant corms in fall for spring blooms. Water deeply after planting; infrequently until bloom; no water after bloom.

# Daffodil

*Narcissus* spp. and hybrids

**ALL ZONES.** Daffodils, native to northern Africa and Europe, grow on rocky hillsides, meadows, riverbanks, grasslands, and woodlands. Leafless stems pop up in late winter to early spring and summer, holding six-petaled double and single blooms with trumpet centers. Hundreds of hybrids in yellow, white, orange, pink, and peach, with contrasting petals and centers. **SIZE (H × W):** 3-inch minis to 20-inch stems x spreading. **SUN:** Full sun to part shade. **MULCH:** River rock, wood chips, shavings. **LANDSCAPE USE:** Plant singly in rock gardens, in masses on hillsides, in meadows, interplant in lawns, cutting gardens, and color borders. Daffodils hold nutrients they need within their bulbs; plant, water deeply, walk away. Dig the area and scatter the bulbs, set them upright, and bury for naturalizing planting. Bulbs are available in fall for spring, summer blooms.

# Daylily

*Hemerocallis* spp.

**ZONES:** 3–10. Hundreds of evergreen, semi-evergreen, and deciduous hybrids grow naturally in shade in mountain ranges and forests, and in full sun in valleys and meadows in China, Japan, and Korea. *Straplike* leaves cluster at the base of plants where strong stems, ranging from 6-inch dwarfs to stately plants 24-inches-tall, hold lilylike ruffled blooms measuring 2 to 4 inches across. Colors are combinations and hues of red, burgundy, rose, yellow, orange, and apricot. **SIZE (H × W):** 6 to 36 inches x 6 to 18 inches, depending on species. **SUN:** Full to part sun. **MULCH:** Chipped bark. **LANDSCAPE USE:** Plant in pots, in drifts along driveway entrances, en masse on hillsides, and in clumps in cutting gardens. Plant deciduous daylily bulbs in fall; evergreen and potted daylilies in spring. Water deeply, infrequently during growing season.

# Drumstick Allium

*Allium* spp.

**ZONES:** 2–10. Drumsticks come from an enormous genus of over 500 members, including chives, garlic, and onions. Native to the northern hemisphere, drumsticks grow in arid locations in dry streambeds, meadows, open fields, and mountain regions. Most are leafless, others have *linear straplike* leaves that lie close to the ground. Magnificent blooms in spring through summer, made up of many tiny flowers (umbels) massed together, form diminutive round globes to baseball-sized orbs in white, pink, fuchsia, blue, purple, lavender, and yellow. **SIZE (H × W):** 6-inches to 5-feet x spreading. **SUN:** Full sun. **MULCH:** Gravel, stone, wood chips, shavings. **LANDSCAPE USE:** Plant in fall, bulb to bulb for a good show in color borders, in drifts at meadow edges, in clumps in cut-flower gardens, in sweeps in bulb beds, tucked into rock gardens. Water deeply after planting, in spring as you see growth.

# Grape Hyacinth

*Muscari* spp.

**ZONES:** 3–9. Grape hyacinth grows on sunny plateaus, rocky hillsides, and meadows and in lightly shaded woodlands in the Mediterranean and southwest Asia. *Lancelike, linear, fleshy, green* to *gray-green leaves* grow at the base of a plant, with short tubular stems sending out lavender-blue, purple, and white hyacinth-like blooms in spring, sometimes repeating in fall. **SIZE (H × W):** Foliage 4 inches across, stems 4 to 12 inches x spreading. **SUN:** Full to part sun. **MULCH:** River rock, chipped or shredded bark. **LANDSCAPE USE:** Plant drifts meandering under the canopy of deciduous trees or along dry streambeds, tucked into rock gardens, in sweeps in the foreground of bulb beds, in color borders interplanted with annuals to take their spot when blooms end. Plant bulbs in fall; divide every three or four years. Water deeply after planting; occasional deep watering in spring.

# Iris

*Iris* spp.

**ZONES:** 3–10. Iris are native to the Northern Hemisphere, growing naturally in the U.S. along the Pacific coast. Hundreds of species. Bearded iris is deciduous to semi-deciduous, with *fanlike sword-shaped leaves*, sending up strong stems in spring, flowers with fuzzy beards, often repeating bloom in fall, some scented or with variegated foliage. Pacific Coast iris naturalize in dry, frost-free areas. Divide iris every three years in fall for rejuvenation. **SIZE (H × W):** Dwarfs 8-inches to standards at 4 feet x spreading. **SUN:** Full to part sun. **MULCH:** Shredded or chipped bark. **LANDSCAPE USE:** Plant single specimens in pots, en masse in cutting gardens, in sweeps in shade, and in drifts in the back of color borders. Water infrequently, deeply during growing season, little to none winter watering.

# Peonies

*Paeonia* spp.

**ZONES:** 3–8. Peonies, which originate from Europe, East Asia, China, and North America, grow in rocky outcrops, in tree understories in woodland areas, at meadow edges tucked among tall grasses, and in the shade of native scrub. *Deeply cut, green* to *silver,* or *gray-green* foliage lines strong stalks on bushy plants. By early spring, bold ruffled, single, or double blooms appear, some scented, in bright red, soft pink, shades of yellow, white, purple, lavender, peach, some varieties with striped petals, multicolored centers, and blends. **SIZE (H × W):** 28 to 36 inches x as wide. **SUN:** Part to full sun. **MULCH:** Chipped, shredded bark. **LANDSCAPE USE:** Plant center stage in the shady understory of deciduous or evergreen trees, in containers in seating areas (for their scent), in groupings in cut-flower gardens, and perennial borders. Water deeply when growth appears in spring; deep, infrequent watering thereafter.

# Squill

*Scilla* spp.

**ALL ZONES.** Squill are native to colder climates of Europe and Asia, temperate regions of Africa, and the Mediterranean. They naturalize in meadows, grasslands, rocky hillsides, woodlands, and seashore settings. Purple to blue, lavender, white, and pink star- or bell-shaped flowers emerge in late winter to early spring on bare stems rising above *lancelike, narrow leaves.* **SIZE (H × W):** 3 to 12 inches depending on species x spreading. **SUN:** Full sun to part shade. **MULCH:** Shredded or chipped bark. **LANDSCAPE USE:** Plant shorter-stemmed types in the understories of trees, in lawns, meadows, and at the front of color borders. Plant taller types in drifts in bulb beds, cut-flower gardens, and perennial gardens. Plant in fall. Deep, infrequent watering during the growing season if no rain/snow. Most are summer dormant or grow slowly in summer in temperate climates, so no watering then.

# Tulip

*Tulipa* spp.

**ZONES:** 4–6; Zones 7–10 require pre-chilling. Over 100 species and thousands of hybrids are classified into 15 groups/divisions. They originated in Europe, Asia, and the Middle East, growing in open areas with cold winters and dry summers. Leaves are *linear* or ovate, *hairy* or smooth, growing at the base of the plant with tall stems holding cup-shaped blooms in every color except blue. **SIZE (H × W):** 6 to 26 inches x clumping. **SUN:** Full sun. **MULCH:** Shredded or chipped wood. **LANDSCAPE USE:** Diminutive types are suitable for rock gardens and the front of garden borders; use taller, boisterous types in pots, in sweeps along driveways, and in masses in cutting gardens. Early fall to late winter planting for blooms in late winter and spring. Water deeply, infrequently during their growing season.

# Honeysuckle

*Lonicera* spp.

**ZONES:** 4–10. Honeysuckle, native to China, Europe, Asia, and southern and eastern U.S., grow in a range of conditions from rocky sites to woodlands. Leaves are green or *gray-green, glossy* to smooth, with tubular, often scented blooms in yellow, salmon, pink, white, and red, covering vines in early spring through summer. **LENGTH:** 15 to 20 feet with support. **SUN:** Full sun to part shade. **MULCH:** Shredded or chipped bark. **LANDSCAPE USE:** *L. japonica* is the most invasive, though used extensively for erosion control in large areas. Others are contained and make good trellis, pergola, fence, and wall coverings, green screens, open area and slope groundcovers. Site scented types upwind! Water monthly in spring and summer. Deciduous or evergreen twining vines—deciduous types don't need water in winter; evergreen types grow slowly and need water only during extended periods without rain.

# Horehound

*Marrubium* spp.

**ZONES:** 4–9. Silver-edged horehound grows in sunny, open, rocky areas of Europe, Asia, Turkey, and the Mediterranean. Grown for attractive *fuzzy coated, green leaves* with *white* to *silver undersides, curling upward* to outline the leaves in silver; they are evergreen. **SIZE (H × W):** 10 inches x 18 inches. **SUN:** Full sun. **MULCH:** River rock, sand, gravel. **LANDSCAPE USE:** Silver-edged horehound's mounding habit makes it a good rock garden plant. Plant in drifts in color borders to accent all other colors. A standalone plant in the night garden, its silver undersides will glow. Plant horehound en masse for a carpet of silver groundcover, use as a filler in containers, plant to meander in and out of taller perennials, interplant in succulent gardens. Deep watering once a month summer to fall and if no rain/snow in winter.

# Ivy

*Hedera* spp.

**ZONES:** 4–10. There are only a dozen species of ivy, which is native to China, Korea, Japan, western Europe, North Africa, and Canary Islands, but hundreds of cultivars offering variations in leaf shapes, patterns, and colors. A trailing evergreen vine growing in part, full shade or full sun, ivy shows changes in leaf shape at maturity (at 10 years), going from *deeply lobed, fan,* or *curly edged* to heart-shaped or ovate. Creamy clusters of flowers on older species lead to deep purple, orange, yellow, or black berries. They climb trees, but are not parasitic. **LENGTH:** Unchecked and given support, over 60 feet. **SUN:** Full sun to full shade. **MULCH:** Bark (when young). **LANDSCAPE USE:** Use smaller types (to 18 inches) in containers, for textural contrast in color borders; use longer as groundcover or as a vine. Look for less invasive cultivars. Monthly deep watering after establishment.

# Periwinkle

*Vinca minor*

**ZONES:** 4–9. Evergreen periwinkle, native to Europe, southern Russia, and the Mediterranean, grows naturally in woodlands. *Glossy*, green leaves, some *variegated*, grow on strong stems that root along the ground as they trail, making vinca a good choice for slopes and hills for erosion control. From midspring through fall, deep purple to blue-violet, lavender, or white five-petaled flowers grow above the foliage. *V. minor* has less tendency to escape its boundaries, but controlled pruning keeps it in check. **SIZE (H × W):** 6 inches x trailing as permitted. **SUN:** Full sun to part shade. **MULCH:** Bark when just planted; none at maturity. **LANDSCAPE USE:** Use for year-round greenery as a groundcover on slopes, in open sunny areas, and in tree understories; denser shade means more foliage, fewer blooms. Makes a good hanging basket. Deep, infrequent monthly watering spring to fall.

# Silver Lace Vine

*Polygonum aubertii*

**ZONES:** 4–10. Silver lace vine is a deciduous native to China. It has *small* heart-shaped leaves, densely growing on seemingly delicate stems that climb and twine up trees and structures. Silver lace sends out abundant clusters of sweetly scented, clear white, lacy blooms from July through September. **LENGTH:** 12 to 15 feet (in one season) to 25 feet. **SUN:** Full sun. **MULCH:** Chipped or shredded bark. **LANDSCAPE USE:** Also called mile-a-minute vine because of its vigor and quick cover. Give it a wire network to climb and get a narrow bed for its roots, and it will gain momentum and form a green screen in one year. Cover an arbor or trellis with greenery and blooms throughout spring and summer or plant in big areas where nothing else grows. No water after establishment. Control growth by pruning heavily anytime.

# Trumpet Vine

*Campsis* **spp.**

**ZONES:** 5–10. The two species of deciduous trumpet vine are native to the eastern U.S. and China. Green leaves are divided into *toothed leaflets*, coming out of dormancy quickly in early spring. The real show is the large, orange-red trumpet, tropical-like blooms growing in clusters from late summer to autumn, attracting every hummingbird in site. Cultivars come in yellow or salmon blooms. **LENGTH:** Quick sprawl to 30 feet after they rebound from pruning. **SUN:** Full sun to part shade. **MULCH:** Chipped, shredded bark. **LANDSCAPE USE:** Plant just one vine to cover an arbor and climb a trellis; just two will cover a large area. Trumpet vine sends out aerial roots that can attach to the home, so it's better to give them their own supports. Prune rampant vines to a few main supports in early spring to refresh. Deep watering after establishment; then deep watering only in drought.

# Virginia Creeper

*Parthenocissus* spp.

**ZONES:** 3–9. Virginia creeper (also Boston ivy) is native to China, Korea, Japan, the Rocky Mountains, and eastern U.S., growing naturally in forests. Semi-deciduous in temperate climates, deciduous in colder areas, Virginia creeper has green, *deeply lobed* or *finely divided leaves*, turning brilliant orange to red in fall. Insignificant blooms produce clusters of black berries that birds love. **LENGTH:** Climbing or sprawling 30 to 60 feet. **SUN:** Full sun to full shade. **MULCH:** Chipped or shredded wood shavings. **LANDSCAPE USE:** No tying or support needed; they attach by disklike suckers, so keep controlled if near house eaves, windows, door trims, or shingles. Vines are non-invasive, controllable, and can camouflage an otherwise uninteresting wall, form beautiful green screens, cover fences, and make a lush green, then colorful, fall groundcover. No watering after establishment.

# Wisteria

*Wisteria* spp.

**ZONES:** 5–9. The largest wisteria vine in the world, in southern California, is over 100 years old—its canopy covers *one acre*. Growing naturally in Japan, Korea, China, and central and southern U.S., these deciduous vines adapt to most conditions: moist and boggy, or dry and hot. They have *divided leaves* and deep, nitrogen-fixing roots (legumes), flowering with giant clusters of pealike, scented blooms in shades of lilac, white, and pink, before leafing out in spring or in unison, depending on the species. Ornamental pods drip from the vines after flowering. **LENGTH:** To 28 feet-plus, given support. **SUN:** Full to part sun. **MULCH:** Chipped, shredded bark. **LANDSCAPE USE:** Use wisteria for quick, long-living cover over sturdy arbors, pergolas, and fences. Prune regularly to control. Grafted types available in early spring. Deep watering during extended dry periods, after establishment.

# Wormwood

*Artemisia* spp. and cultivars

**ZONES:** 3–9. Wormwood naturally grows in arid open fields, scrubs, and prairies in Europe, Asia, the Mediterranean, and across the U.S. It is grown for its *high oil content*, evergreen foliage, *finely divided, feathery, white, silver* to *gray-green*, but some types bloom in white, yellow, or cream early spring through summer. **SIZE (H × W):** 6 to 30 inches x 1 to 12 feet, depending on species. **SUN:** Full sun. **MULCH:** Gravel, stone, sand, chipped or shredded bark. **LANDSCAPE USE:** A somewhat gnarled growth habit, with mature trunks becoming shredded with age, wormwood can be planted along slopes for effective erosion control, in groupings in the perennial bed, in masses in prairie-style gardens, in drifts for a textural ground cover. Cultivars are least invasive. Water after established only during extended drought.

# Bermudagrass

*Cynodon dactylon*

**ZONES:** 7–10. Bermudagrass, native to South Africa, is a warm-season grass, rapidly spreading by both surface stolons and underground rhizomes as temperatures rise. A very dense, high-traffic, drought- and heat-tolerant lawn, it can be invasive, so containment is necessary. Bermudagrass goes dormant in extended drought, quickly recovering when given any amount of water. It is *fine bladed*, growing close to the surface, choking out any weeds that might try to grow with it. Turning straw-brown in autumn, some more cold-tolerant varieties have been developed. **MOW HEIGHT:** ½ to 1½ inches depending on variety. **SUN:** Full sun. **LANDSCAPE USE:** Use for lawns, paths where invasion is not an issue; used for grazing in the South. Plant from seed, sod, or stolons spring through summer. Seeded lawns need less mowing. After establishment, minimal monthly watering during summer; fertilize once in spring.

# Blue Grama Grass

*Bouteloua gracilis*

**ZONES:** 3–10. Blue grama grass is called mosquito grass because the flower spikes hover mosquito-like on top of the stems. A clumping grass with *thin, linear gray-green blades* that spread by surface rhizomes and reseeding, it has fed many buffalo roaming North America's prairies and grasslands. Turning a dormant amber during winter, it sends out new tufts in early spring that quickly green up. **MOW HEIGHT:** 1½ inches for a more manicured lawn or allow to grow to 1 foot for meadows or prairies. **SUN:** Full sun. **LANDSCAPE USE:** If unmowed, it sends out 24-inch spikes holding brown-purple tinted flower heads holding many seeds that sway gently in the breeze. Sow by seed in fall to take advantage of winter rains or snow. Water deeply the first year to 1 foot, then supplemental monthly watering in subsequent summers; no fertilizer.

# Buffalo Grass

*Buchloe dactyloides*

**ZONES:** 3–10. Buffalo grass is native to the U.S., growing from Montana to Arizona. It has *gray-green linear* leaves that turn wheat colored in fall, remaining until plants come out of dormancy in mid-spring. Slow to germinate and fill in, once established it spreads by surface runners that can creep into adjacent flowerbeds, but the invasion is slow so it is easily controlled. **MOW HEIGHT:** Mow for the look of a traditional lawn or allow it to grow freely to 4 inches. **SUN:** Full sun. **LANDSCAPE USE:** New cold-hardy, drought-tough, deeper green, and shorter dormancy cultivars are available in plugs and sod for spring planting, or sow by seed in fall. After germination and establishment, water irregularly but deeply to 1 foot in spring and summer, allowing the soil to dry between waterings; no fertilizer needed.

# Tall Fescue

*Festuca arundinacea*

**ZONES:** 4–7. Tall fescue is native to Europe, North Africa, and northern Asia, but has naturalized in the cooler regions of North America. It is a cool-season grass, keeping its deep green color throughout winter. It is a bunching type, so does not spread by stolons or runners, making it non-invasive. Tall fescue is a *deep rooting grass*, making it drought tolerant, and it has long blades that shade its roots for heat tolerance. **MOW HEIGHT:** 2 to 3 inches for a lawn; if allowed to grow taller it requires less water. **SUN:** Full sun to part shade. **LANDSCAPE USE:** Plant it on a slope and never mow for erosion control. New cultivars and dwarf types available in seed or sod. Water deeply but infrequently once established; supplement in winter if no moisture in temperate zones; fertilize in spring, midsummer.

# Zoysia 'Emerald', 'Meyer'

*Zoysia* cultivars

**ZONES:** 5–11. Zoysia grass is native to Japan, China, and Southeast Asia. A warm-season grass, it spreads slowly by stolons and rhizomes, turns brown after first frost, greening up in early spring. A coarse-textured grass, the *leaves roll into themselves* in heat and drought, conserving moisture. *Deep rooting* 'Emerald' is more wiry in appearance and texture and faster to establish than 'Meyer', which is cold tolerant and slower to go winter dormant. 'Meyer' is softer bladed, resembling Kentucky bluegrass, slower to establish, but tolerates part shade in hotter summer climates. **MOW HEIGHT:** Mow 1 to 2 inches in full sun; taller if shaded. **SUN:** Full to part sun. **LANDSCAPE USE:** Use for lawns, pathways, home putting greens. Use *Z. tenuifolia* for meadow planting. Plant plugs, sow seed spring to early summer. Water deeply, once a week, 6 to 8 inches deep in spring, summer; fertilize spring, late summer.

# Meadows

**ALL ZONES.** Meadows are a landscape alternative for lawns that require regular watering, mowing, and fertilizing. Drought-tolerant grasses make up half of the meadow, with annual wildflowers, perennials, and bulbs filling the rest. Buffalograss, blue grama grass, zoysia, and ornamental grasses such as blue fescue, maidenhair, and muhly grass form the foundation. Seed mixes appropriate for your zone can include poppies, Mexican hat, coreopsis, yarrow, coneflower, penstemon, Russian sage, lupine, hardy geranium, and alyssum. Add bulbs in drifts of daylilies, daffodils, iris, allium, and squill. Building a meadow is a three-year process. Year one: sow in early spring, keep seedbed moist, mow to 12 inches every four weeks to encourage deep roots. Year two: water deeply once a week during summer; mow tall every six weeks. Year three: water deeply once a month, mow in fall after blooming in cold climes, late winter in warmer winters; no fertilizer.

# Blue Fescue

*Festuca glauca*

**ZONES:** 4–11. Blue fescue, native to Europe, is a clumping grass that grows naturally in meadows, grasslands, and woodland edges. An evergreen, it has distinctive *linear, blue-gray, blue-green,* or *silver-white tightly rolled leaves* with blue-green flowers on short 4-inch spikes in summer. **SIZE (H × W):** The species to 12 inches x 10 inches; powder blue 'Elijah Blue' to 8 inches; true blue 'Siskiyou' to 18 inches; chartreuse 'Golden Toupee' to 8 inches for part shade. **SUN:** Full sun to part shade. **MULCH:** Bark, gravel, stone, sand. **LANDSCAPE USE:** Use shorter types in rock gardens and in the foreground of color beds. Plant blocks of blue fescue in formal gardens, drifts in meadows, in masses for a groundcover, and single plants along the "shore" of a dry streambed. Available in quart and gallon pots for spring planting. Water sparingly after established; divide every three years.

# Fountain Grass

*Pennisetum* spp.

**ZONES:** 6–10. Fountain grass grows naturally in savannas, woodland edges, meadows, and grasslands in temperate regions of Asia, Africa, and Australia. A full-sun, clumping, fountain-shaped grass with *linear leaves* in green, *blue-green*; cultivars in purple and mahogany. Spikes of plumes in white, reddish-purple, tan, or black, summer through fall. **SIZE (H × W):** Dwarfs 10 inches x 12 inches; others 2 to 6 feet x as wide. **SUN:** Full sun to shade. **MULCH:** Shredded bark, stone, gravel. **LANDSCAPE USE:** Not frost hardy, but status worthy in the cut flower, cottage garden as a long-season annual; in other areas, use as a focal point in perennial gardens, in drifts in meadows, along dry streambeds, in rock gardens, en masse on hillsides, and in containers. Water deeply to establish, then once monthly; cut flowers before seed set in temperate areas to minimize self-sowing.

# Little Bluestem

*Schizachyrium scoparium*

**ZONES:** 4–9. Little bluestem is native to North America, growing in meadows, rocky hillsides, and prairies. A tightly clumping grass, its *linear leaves* are green, *gray-green, blue-green* that take on fall colors in tan, purple, orange, burgundy, and red, remaining for winter interest. Flowers appear on wispy stalks in late summer in white and are non-showy until fall when they turn silver, making an attractive flower for dried arrangements. **SIZE (H × W):** 3 feet x 1 foot. **SUN:** Full sun. **MULCH:** Stone, sand, river rock. **LANDSCAPE USE:** Use in home meadows, cut-flower gardens, in drifts along dry streambeds, in masses on slopes, and prairie gardens. Water deeply the first year, then deep irregular watering for two years; thereafter, it needs little water other than rain. Not good for small gardens as it reseeds.

# Maidenhair Grass

*Miscanthus sinensis*

**ZONES:** 4–9. Maidenhair grass is from Southeast Asia. A deciduous, clumping grass, with reedlike stems and *narrow, linear leaves*, it grows in a range of conditions from dry meadows to boggy marshes. Grown for its upright, slightly arching habit and flowers, which appear in late summer to fall as tassels in white, silver, bronze, or pink, held high above the foliage. Fall foliage and flowers remain for winter interest. **SIZE (H × W):** Species 10 to 14 feet x 4 feet; dwarfs to 4 feet x as wide. **SUN:** Full sun. **MULCH:** Shredded or chipped bark, gravel, river rock. **LANDSCAPE USE:** Use as a focal point, in groupings for summer screening, as accent for boulders, or in meadows. Available in quart, gallon, or 5-gallon pots for spring planting. Water deeply, infrequently three years to establish; divide to control size in spring; no fertilizer.

# Muhly Grass

*Muhlenbergia* spp.

**ZONES:** 5–9. Muhly grass is native to the U.S. from the lower eastern seaboard, across the Southwest, and into California. It grows on rocky slopes, prairies, and along roadsides. It is a *fine textured*, clumping, warm-season grass with green or *gray-green* foliage. The showstoppers are the feathery flowers that appear on 12-inch-tall stems in pink to pinkish red in late summer to fall, then turn tan, remaining for winter interest. **SIZE (H × W):** 2 to 3 feet x as wide. **SUN:** Full to part sun. **MULCH:** Gravel, river rock. **LANDSCAPE USE:** Use muhly grass as a foreground focal point in perennial gardens, in drifts in prairie gardens or meadows, as accents with boulders, and scattered in rock gardens. Cultivars in quart, gallon, and 5-gallon pots for spring planting. Water deeply to establish, then once every 4 to 6 weeks in summer; no fertilizer.

# Reed Grass

*Calamagrostis* spp.

**ZONES:** 5–9. Reed grass, native to Europe, North America, and Russia, grows in dry, open prairies to wet woodlands. Evergreen, semi-deciduous, and deciduous, depending upon species and selection, it is an all-season clumping grass with green *linear leaves*, some with *variegated green/ white stripes*, sending out upright, uniform airy flowers in pinkish-gray, burgundy, or tan, mid- to late summer, turning wheat-colored in fall, persisting for winter interest. **SIZE (H × W):** 3 to 6 feet x 2 to 3 feet. **SUN:** Full sun to part shade. **MULCH:** Shredded bark, river rock, gravel. **LANDSCAPE USE:** Use in drifts as background screens, singly as a focal point in perennial gardens, or massed in meadows. Water irregularly and deeply to establish the first two years, then deep regular watering every few weeks in summer; shear back in early spring; no fertilizer.

# Blanket Flower

*Gaillardia grandiflora*

**ZONES:** 3–8. Blanket flower grows in prairies and hillsides throughout the west, central, and southern portions of the U.S. *Deeply lobed* or *toothed, hairy leaves* form bushy plants that send out long stems, holding bright ray flowers, from spring until first frost, in yellow and orange tipped in yellow with contrasting cone centers. New cultivars offer maroon and burgundy flowers with contrasting cones. **SIZE (H × W):** 2 to 4 feet x 18 to 24 inches, depending on cultivar. **SUN:** Full sun. **MULCH:** Shredded or chipped bark. **LANDSCAPE USE:** Plant in color borders, mid- or foreground in perennial gardens, in drifts at meadow edges, and in containers. Deadhead for continuous bloom, cut back to 6 inches in early fall in cold climates; new growth overwinters. Sow seed in spring or plant from quart or gallon containers. Deep, infrequent watering.

# Coneflower

*Echinacea* spp.

**ZONES:** 3–9. Coneflower grows naturally in dry meadows and grasslands, rocky hillsides, and prairies in southeast and central U.S. Oval *toothed* or *deeply lobed leaves* are covered with a *stiff, hairy coating.* Tall *hairy stems* rise in early summer to hold daisylike blooms in white, bright pink, purple, yellow, orange, and combinations, with large contrasting cone centers in black, brown, orange, and yellow. **SIZE (H × W):** 2 to 4 feet x 18 to 24 inches. **SUN:** Full sun. **MULCH:** Chipped or shredded bark; river rock. **LANDSCAPE USE:** Use coneflower en masse in cut-flower or perennial gardens, in drifts in meadows, singly in containers, on dry hillsides, and in rock gardens. It doesn't care to be disturbed once planted, but reseeds to naturalize if seed cones remain on plants. Sow seed or plant quart or gallon containers in spring. Deep, infrequent watering.

# Flax

*Phormium* hybrids

**ZONES:** 9–10. Flax comes from rocky hillsides, scrub areas, and riverbanks in New Zealand. Grown for its foliage that is *narrow, linear, sheathlike, folded slightly inward,* and growing in fans that form a vase shape. Long leaves in shades of dark green and white contrasting stripes, or in mahogany, plum, red, or blackish-red leaves with pink or yellow stripes. Some shades turn deeper in cooler weather. Mature plants bloom spring to late summer. Tall, dramatic stems reach 12 feet, with yellow-green or reddish tubular blooms. **SIZE (H × W):** 2 to 8 feet x 2 to 8 feet. **SUN:** Full to part sun. **MULCH:** Sand, gravel, rock, shredded bark. **LANDSCAPE USE:** Grow in masses poolside, in sweeps on slopes, as background in perennial gardens, or as a dramatic container plant; overwinter indoors in colder climates. Sold in 4-inch, quart, or gallon pots; water sparingly.

# Hummingbird Mint

*Agastache* spp.

**ZONES:** 4–10. Hummingbird mint is native to China, Japan, Mexico, and the U.S., growing in dry open grasslands, rocky slopes, and meadows. *Spicy, licorice-scented, glossy* green or *gray-green* leaves grow on bushy plants, sending out flower spikes from midsummer to autumn in pink, purple, orange, blue, yellow, purple, apricot, and combinations; hummingbird and butterfly magnet. **SIZE (H × W):** 18 inches to 6 feet x 12 inches to 36 inches, depending on cultivar. **SUN:** Full to part sun. **MULCH:** Chipped or shredded bark. **LANDSCAPE USE:** Use hummingbird mint singly as a focal point, planted in drifts in prairie gardens or meadow edges, and in containers. Plant in spring from quart or gallon containers; cut back in fall in warm-winter areas, in early spring in colder climes; deep, infrequent watering after established, minimal to no water in winter.

# Hummingbird Trumpet

*Zauschneria californica*

**ZONES:** 8–10. Hummingbird trumpet is native to the western U.S. and Mexico, growing on dry slopes and coastal chaparral areas. Typically sprawling, leaves are *lancelike, hairy, gray-* to *silver-green.* The real show are the flowers that are bright, fiery orange to red and funnel shaped for the hummingbirds, covering the plant from late summer to autumn. **SIZE (H × W):** 6 to 48 inches x 3 to 4 feet, depending on the many cultivars. **SUN:** Full sun. **MULCH:** Rock, stone, sand. **LANDSCAPE USE:** Use hummingbird trumpet in rock gardens, in drifts on slopes or in meadows, en masse to drip over rock walls, or in perennial or color borders. Water deeply once a month after establishment. Control ranginess after second year by cutting back to 3 inches in fall; pinch in spring to promote bushiness.

# Lamb's Ear

*Stachys* spp.

**ZONES:** 5–9. Lamb's ear grows in a range of conditions from streamsides and open forests to dry, rocky scrublands; meadows; and hillsides in southwestern U.S., Greece, Turkey, Iran, and Europe. Often matting, sometimes tall and bushy, with *thick* leaves, often *aromatic* (some like it, some don't!), usually *furry,* green with *lighter* or *white undersides, deeply veined,* with *slightly curled* or *toothed* edges. Short spikes of tubular blooms in pink, yellow, red, white, or purple appear in late spring. **SIZE (H × W):** 6 to 36 inches x 12 to 48 inches. **SUN:** Full sun to part shade. **MULCH:** Rock, gravel, shredded or chipped bark. **LANDSCAPE USE:** Use shorter types in drifts as groundcover in perennial beds, color borders, in rock gardens, bushy forms as focal point, in midground meadows, hills, and in containers. Plant containers in spring; deep, infrequent watering, less in winter.

# Lavender

*Lavendula* spp.

**ZONES:** 5–10. Lavender is native to the Mediterranean, South Africa, Canary Islands, and Spain; grows in exposed and rocky sites. It is evergreen, slowing or stopping growth in colder climates, then refoliating in spring. Lavender is grown for its aromatic (*high in oils*), green or *gray-green small, linear* leaves that are *toothed or serrated,* and sometimes *softly hairy*. Scented blooms in purple, lavender, pink, and white grow on short (3-inch) or long (to 3 foot) stalks in late spring. Continuous blooming year-round in temperate zones. **SIZE (H × W):** 1 to 4 feet x 1 to 3 feet. **SUN:** Full sun. **MULCH:** Rock, gravel, sand. **LANDSCAPE USE:** Grow in pots in colder climates; overwinter indoors. Grow in sweeps in the perennial garden, in blocks for formal garden, in drifts in the meadow, as filler in the color border. Available in pots year-round, many cultivars. Water irregularly, deeply.

# Maximilian Sunflower

*Helianthus maximilianii*

**ZONES:** 4–9. Maximilian sunflower grows in open meadows and grasslands of the central and southwestern U.S. It is clumping, tall-stemmed, and covered with *long, rough,* deep green leaves, and it spreads by rhizomes. Tall, strong stems late summer through fall, 3-inch bright yellow sunflowers on short stems line the stalks, creating a bushy floral show. Flowers persist, turning brown for winter interest. **SIZE (H × W):** 10 feet x 3 feet. **SUN:** Full sun. **MULCH:** Chipped or shredded bark. **LANDSCAPE USE:** Use as a spring, summer, or fall green screen, in the background of perennial gardens, along meadow edges, or lining fencelines. Cut back to the ground in spring when there is new green growth or divide to control the spread. Plant in spring from containers. After first year establishment, water deeply once a month if no summer rains.

# Penstemon

*Penstemon* spp.

**ZONES:** 3–10. Penstemon grows in a broad range of conditions and climates in the U.S. Deciduous, partly or fully evergreen, bushy to linear shrubs grow in arid desert, prairie, grassland, woodland, and alpine regions. Over 250 species and many cultivars make diverse leaf types, *narrow,* ovate, *leathery, shiny, waxy*, green, and *gray-green*, forming at the base of the plant, whirling up the long stems or with leafless stems supporting tubular blooms in red, pink, purple, white, and orange in summer through fall. **SIZE (H × W):** 4 to 40 inches x 8 to 36 inches, depending on type. **SUN:** Full sun to part shade. **MULCH:** Shredded or chipped bark, gravel, sand, rock. **LANDSCAPE USE:** Use in wildflower, meadow, or prairie gardens; in sweeps in perennial borders; in drifts along driveways. Available in quart, gallon, 5-gallon pots in spring; allow soil to dry before watering deeply, infrequently.

# Red Yucca

*Hesperaloe parvifola*

**ZONES:** 8–10. Red yucca is native to Texas and New Mexico, growing in arid locations. Red yucca has the body of a yucca with tough, *linear leaves with fibrous edges* forming rosettes at plant base. Aloe-like flowers on 5-foot-long stems grow out of the base and are covered with tubular, deep to bright red and coral blooms, late spring into fall. **SIZE (H × W):** Flower stalks to 5 feet x 3 to 4 feet clumps. **SUN:** Full sun. **MULCH:** Gravel, rock, stone, or sand. **LANDSCAPE USE:** In cold climates, grow in a pot; overwinter indoors. Where hardy, cluster red yucca in the midground of desert scenes, singly as focal points, along dry streambeds, in drifts in dry perennial beds. Water irregularly and deeply to establish; no winter watering; thereafter water deeply twice monthly during summer.

# Russian sage

*Perovskia atriplicifolia*

**ZONES:** 5–9. Russian sage is native to the Himalayas and central Asia, growing naturally in rocky locations. Evergreen, vase-shaped, and shrubby, it has white stems, covered in *silver to gray-green deeply cut, aromatic* leaves. Small tubular, purple, lavender, and violet-blue airy flowers form in masses in late spring and summer. **SIZE (H × W):** 2 to 3 feet x as wide. **SUN:** Full sun. **MULCH:** Rock, gravel, sand, wood chip. **LANDSCAPE USE:** Use Russian sage in perennial borders, in masses in prairie or meadow gardens, in sweeps on slopes, along driveways. Available in gallon pots in spring; spreads by runners to colonize, so plant half what is needed to fill a space. New cultivars are smaller, more compact, and less apt to become invasive. Water deeply, infrequently, allowing soil to dry before watering to establish; thereafter, water only in long droughts.

# Salvia

*Salvia* spp.

**ZONES:** 5–11 Salvia has over 900 species, with cultivars for every landscape. Grows naturally in temperate and tropical regions worldwide on rocky, dry hillsides, in meadows, woodlands, and moist grasslands. Evergreen, bushy salvia *contain oils*, have *linear* or oval leaves, with *toothed* or *notched edges*, in all hues of green, *gray-green*, or *silvery white with white undersides* and *fuzzy leaf coatings*. Spring through fall blooms on spikes, tubular flowers in shades of red, orange, purple, blue, lavender, pink, white. **SIZE (H × W):** 1 to 5 feet x 1 to 6 feet. **SUN:** Full sun to part shade. **MULCH:** Rock, gravel, shredded or chipped bark. **LANDSCAPE USE:** Plant en masse on slopes; in prairie, woodland, or rock gardens; in drifts in perennial cutting gardens. Where not hardy, use as season-long annual color in containers. Plant containers in spring; allow soil to dry between deep, infrequent waterings.

# Speedwell

*Veronica* spp.

**ZONES:** 3–8. Speedwell comes from temperate areas of Europe, Asia, and the Mediterranean, growing in dry meadows, rocky hillsides, and partly sunny woodlands. Matlike in growth, leaves are deep to mid-green, or *silvery white, crinkled, deeply veined, lobed,* or *serrated, waxy,* or *woolly,* depending on species. Flowers bloom on short stems, in white, purple, blue, rosy pink, lavender, and red; in spring or summer, some into fall. **SIZE (H × W):** 3 to 24 inches x 12 to 24 inches. **SUN:** Full to part sun. **MULCH:** Shredded or chipped bark, river rock. **LANDSCAPE USE:** Deciduous in cold climes and evergreen elsewhere, speedwell is a good groundcover on hills and slopes, in sweeps in the front of borders, in groups in rock gardens, and in containers. Plant containers in spring. Water deeply to establish, then infrequent summer watering, little to no watering in winter.

# Tickseed

*Coreopsis* spp.

**ZONES:** 3–9. Tickseed grows naturally in meadows, prairies, and woodlands in North and Central America and Mexico. Deep green, sometimes *fuzzy, deeply lobed* leaves form clumps that spread by rhizomes. Tall flower stems hold daisy-like flowers beginning late spring into summer and fall, in yellow and orange-yellow, cultivars in red, pink, lavender, cream, and combinations. In very cold climates, tickseed is often used as a long-blooming annual; it reseeds and can naturalize in other areas. **SIZE (H × W):** 9 inches to 4 feet x 8 to 36 inches, depending on type. **SUN:** Full sun. **MULCH:** Chipped or shredded bark. **LANDSCAPE USE:** Use coreopsis singly in pots, in drifts in the meadow, in groups in the perennial garden, and in masses in the prairie or cottage garden. Sow seed or plant from quart or gallon containers in spring. Deep, infrequent watering.

# Yarrow

*Achillea* spp.

**ZONES:** 3–9. Yarrow grows naturally in Europe, Asia, and North America in meadows and dry grasslands to (partly shady) moist mountain ranges. Deciduous to semi-deciduous, spreading by runners to form a dense mat, yarrow varies from tall upright forms with aromatic (*oils*), *deeply divided, gray-green, fuzzy* leaves to short, mat-forming types with *linear, toothed* deep green leaves. Tight clusters of daisy-like flowers summer through fall in yellow and white, many cultivars in red, hot to pale pink, lavender, and orange. **MATURE SIZE (H × W):** 6 to 36 inches x 9 to 24 inches. **SUN:** Full sun to part shade. **MULCH:** Chipped or shredded bark. **LANDSCAPE USE:** Plant yarrow en masse as a turf alternative, on slopes, in drifts in color borders, cut-flower gardens, and prairie, meadow, and cottage gardens. Plant in spring from seed, stolons, or containers. Water to establish, then infrequently during summer; none if winter dormant.

# Barberry

*Berberis* spp.

**ZONES:** 3–9. Barberry grows in rocky, mountain locations throughout China and South America. It is evergreen or deciduous, having small oval, *glossy* and sometimes *spiny* leaves and stems. In colder climates, brilliant fall colors appear in bronze, red, burgundy, and orange. Bright yellow to orange, cup-shaped blooms blanket cascading and arching branches in spring, followed by red, blue, to black berries in fall, persisting into winter. Barberry spreads by runners; species could become invasive in temperate climates. **SIZE (H × W):** 1 to 10 feet x 2 to 15 feet. **SUN:** Full sun to part shade. **MULCH:** Chipped or shredded bark. **LANDSCAPE USE:** Select from the many cultivars or non-fruit-bearing types. Use low-growing types for groundcovers on slopes; taller, for screens, focal points, or background plantings. Prune evergreens in fall to shape; prune deciduous in winter. Deep, irregular waterings.

# Butterfly Bush

*Buddleja* spp.

**ZONES:** 5–10. Butterfly bush, native to Asia, Africa, North and South America, and China, grows in rocky and scrub locations. Evergreen, semi-evergreen, and deciduous shrubs have arching stems that cascade to the ground, covered in *lance-shaped, roughly textured*, or *hairy* green or *gray-green* leaves. Clusters of tubular, fragrant flowers at the growing tips in bright to pale pink, lavender to purple, orange to yellow, and white occur late winter, early spring, and summer, depending upon the species. **SIZE (H × W):** 5 to 20 feet x as wide. **SUN:** Full sun. **MULCH:** Chipped or shredded bark. **LANDSCAPE USE:** Use butterfly bush in perennial beds as focal points, as midground or background plantings, in drifts along a drive; use smaller types in large containers. Prune back hard after bloom, to the ground in early spring in colder climates. Plant containers in spring. Water deeply; let soil dry between waterings.

# Chaste Tree

*Vitex agnus-castus*

**ZONES:** 5–9. Chaste tree is grown as a small tree, but naturally it is a large shrub, growing in dry streambeds in the Mediterranean and central Asia. Deciduous, it has *deeply cut palmate* (like the palm of your hand), *aromatic* green leaves, with sprays of small tubular flowers in purple, lavender, and white, late summer to fall. The lightly scented blooms are attractive to pollinators. **SIZE (H × W):** 6 to 25 feet x as wide. **SUN:** Full sun. **MULCH:** Chipped or shredded bark, gravel, rock. **LANDSCAPE USE:** Use chaste tree as a focal point, to anchor an entrance, plant in groups for a screen or in the background to surround a landscape bed. Because of its bee magnet capabilities, site it away from gathering spots. Either prune hard or cut to the ground each year for new soft growth; minimal watering after establishment.

# Cotoneaster

*Cotoneaster* spp.

**ZONES:** 4–9. Semi-evergreen, evergreen, or deciduous cotoneaster are native to woodland and rocky areas of North Africa, Asia, and China. Low-growing and large, dense types have long arching branches covered in small, oval, *shiny* or dull, *deeply veined* or *wavy edged* leaves. Profuse white to pink cup-shaped flowers cover shrubs spring to summer, followed by orange-red berries. Deciduous types put on a fall show of pinks, red, and orange foliage. **SIZE (H × W):** Dwarf is 4 to 8 inches x 12 inches to 10 feet; shrub is 2 to 15 feet x 6 to 15 feet. **SUN:** Full sun to part shade. **MULCH:** Shredded or chipped bark. **LANDSCAPE USE:** Use shorter types as groundcovers and in rock gardens. Use taller shrubs as background plantings, focal points, natural hedgerows and screening. Plant containers in spring. Give them room; no pruning. Water deeply, infrequently to establish; once monthly during summer thereafter.

# Crape myrtle

*Lagerstroemia indica*

**ZONES:** 5–9. Deciduous crape myrtle grows naturally in China's woodlands. They are known for their long bloom period, from summer through fall; fall foliage in colder climates, green turning brilliant red; and their *peeling bark* at maturity. Foliage is *small, shiny*, and oval, blooms are large clusters of tiny crepelike flowers in white and shades of pink, red, and purple. **SIZE (H × W):** Up to 20 feet tall x as wide; many cultivars 3 to 4 feet x as wide. **SUN:** Full sun. **MULCH:** Shredded or chipped bark. **LANDSCAPE USE:** Crape myrtle makes a showy green and floral screen, a focal point, or use in drifts in perennial beds. Train as small lawn trees or grow in containers. Species grows slowly. No pruning except for crossing limbs; deep, infrequent water. In Zones 5 and 6, they may die to the ground in winter, but come back in early spring.

# Euonymus

*Euonymus* spp.

**ZONES:** 2–9. Euonymus herald from Asia, growing in woodland thickets. They are evergreen, semi-, or fully deciduous, and notable for their foliage: green, *variegated with white*, oval, *toothed*, or *scalloped*, turning to brilliant fall colors of bright to pinkish red. Spring and summer flowers are inconspicuous compared to the fruits that form in fall that are winged, lobed, and often two-toned in pink and yellow or red and orange. **SIZE (H × W):** Low is 2 feet x 15 feet; climbers are 2 feet x indefinite; shrubs are 3 to 12 feet x 3 to 15 feet. **SUN:** Full sun to full shade. **MULCH:** Shredded or chipped bark. **LANDSCAPE USE:** Use low shrubs as groundcovers, climbing types for vines, taller forms for background, screening, or green walls. Prune hard for formal; otherwise, only to cut out dead or damaged branches in winter for deciduous and after blooming for evergreen. Deep, infrequent water.

# Heavenly Bamboo

*Nandina domestica*

**ZONES:** 6–9. Heavenly bamboo, a semi- to evergreen shrub, is native to China, India, and Japan, growing in mountain valleys. Grown for its beautiful, *linear, lacy, deeply cut* green foliage, new growth in pinkish red, deeper purplish-red to red in cooler fall temperatures. It grows by canes, reminiscent of bamboo, spreading by non-invasive sucker growth. Large, white clusters of small star-shaped flowers form in spring to summer, followed by bright red berries that persist into winter. **SIZE (H × W):** Species, 6 feet x 5 feet; cultivars, 1 to 4 feet x 2 to 6 feet. **SUN:** Full sun to full shade. **MULCH:** Shredded or chipped bark. **LANDSCAPE USE:** Use for outdoor room enclosures, in Japanese gardens, as screening in small gardens, groupings in midground shrub beds, in containers. Prune by cutting older canes to the ground; infrequent deep water.

# Indian Hawthorn

*Rhaphiolepis* spp.

**ZONES:** 7–11. Evergreen Indian hawthorn is native to China, Japan, and Korea, growing in scrubs. Grown as a small tree (*R.* 'Majestic Beauty') or as a medium-sized shrub, Indian hawthorn has *glossy, leathery, slightly serrated leaf edges* on a bushy, compact form. Spring, summer, or fall blooms (depending upon species) are small, star-shaped flowers in clusters, pale pink to deep rosy pink or red, some lightly scented. Hybrids offer fall foliage color and some disease resistance. **SIZE (H × W):** 2 to 6 feet x 2 to 8 feet. **SUN:** Full sun to part shade. **MULCH:** Shredded or chipped bark. **LANDSCAPE USE:** Use Indian hawthorn as a low hedge, in sweeps in the midground landscape, as background green screens in small gardens, in groupings on hillsides, and containers. No pruning; infrequent, deep watering, less in winter.

# Lilac

*Syringa* spp. and hybrids

**ZONES:** 3–8. Deciduous lilac grows naturally from southeastern Europe to eastern Asia in scrub and woodland habitats. Favored for its heavenly scented clusters of blooms in white, cream pink, and purple pastels from mid- to late spring, depending upon type. It is an upright to arching, bushy shrub, covered in green, oval- to *lance-shaped* leaves. **SIZE (H × W):** Most species grow 5 to 15 feet x as wide; *S. reticulata* 30 feet x 20 feet. **SUN:** Full sun to part shade. **MULCH:** Shredded or chipped bark. **LANDSCAPE USE:** Use it for a natural hedge, seasonal green screen, in perennial or cut-flower gardens, or as a focal point shrub. Hybrids in varying flower colors, shrub sizes, and heat tolerance are available. No pruning, but deadhead after bloom; stop watering after bloom; resume deep, infrequent watering in spring when you see regrowth.

# Manzanita

*Arctostaphylos* spp.

**ZONES:** 2–10. Manzanita grow in colonies on rocky hillsides, mountain draws, and coastal scrubs in California and western North America up to Alaska. Evergreen (except *A. alpina*) manzanita are prostrate and wide branching, with smooth red bark at maturity. The leaves are *fleshy,* some *glossy,* oval or *toothed, green with white undersides* or *gray-green.* Flowering late winter to early spring in clusters of small, upside-down urns in pink or white, followed by red or brown berries. **SIZE (H × W):** 4 inches to 20 feet x 3 to 20 feet, depending upon selection. **SUN:** Full sun. **MULCH:** Gravel, shredded or chipped bark. **LANDSCAPE USE:** Manzanita makes a good groundcover on hillsides, focal point shrub, clusters in woodland gardens, rock garden plant in cool summers. Plant containers in spring. Water deeply to establish; thereafter, once monthly during hot summers, twice monthly in cooler summers; no pruning.

# Mock Orange

*Philadelphus* spp.

**ZONES:** 3–9. Deciduous mock orange grows on rocky and scrubby slopes and hillsides in Europe, Asia, and North and Central America. It gets its name from the citrus-scented blooms that cover the plant in late spring to early summer. Mock orange has slightly or pronounced arching stems covered in green, oval, *deeply veined* leaves. **SIZE (H × W):** 1 to 10 feet x 2 to 10 feet, depending upon type. **SUN:** Full sun to part shade. **MULCH:** Shredded or chipped bark. **LANDSCAPE USE:** Grow as a seasonal, scented green screen, in sweeps through the perennial bed, as a focal point, drifts on gentle slopes, as background or midground plantings in woodland gardens and used singly in containers. After flowering, cut old growth out to the ground; shear old shrubs to the ground to rejuvenate. Infrequent deep watering; supplement in winter if no moisture.

# Rosewood

*Vauquelinia* spp.

**ZONES:** 5–10. Rosewood is a hardy, large, evergreen shrub native to scrub outbacks of Arizona, California, and Baja Mexico. Reminiscent of oleander, with a similar growth habit and leaf shape, rosewood has a deep green leaf with *lighter undersides* and *serrated leaf edges* but is non-poisonous. Clusters of bright white flowers form in late spring through fall when they turn to tan seed capsules that persist into winter for foraging birds. Slow growing, but once established, requires no further care. **SIZE (H × W):** 5 to 25 feet x 5 to 15 feet. **SUN:** Full sun to part shade. **MULCH:** Shredded or chipped bark. **LANDSCAPE USE:** Use en masse to line a drive, screen a view, or form a hedgerow. No pruning. Water deeply, infrequently the first three years; thereafter, no watering required except to encourage faster growth.

# Serviceberry

*Amelanchier* spp.

**ZONES:** 4–9. Native to the western and eastern U.S., China, Korea, and Japan; grows in woodlands. Deciduous, with *gray-white* oval to oblong leaves, some *fuzzy-coated* when juvenile, turning yellow, red, orange, or purple in autumn. Mid- to late spring blooms are clear white or pale pink and hang in clusters, some fragrant. Red, blue-black berries form, edible for people and wildlife. **SIZE (H × W):** Compact types 6 feet x as wide; species 25 feet x as wide. **SUN:** Full sun to part shade. **MULCH:** Shredded or chipped bark. **LANDSCAPE USE:** Show it off by placing it midground in front of evergreens, in groups as a border, or as a focal point. Slow grower; some spread by suckering. No pruning or fertilizing; water deeply, infrequently the first three springs and summers, then monthly during summer, more for quicker growth.

# Sumac

*Rhus* spp.

**ZONES:** 2–10. Sumac grows naturally in dry streambeds and rocky slopes in the southwest and eastern U.S. Evergreen or deciduous; leaves range from oval, *linear*, and *divided* in green, *gray-green*, some fragrant (or odoriferous!). Deciduous types have brilliant fall colors in yellow, orange, and red. In early spring, small, pink, yellow, or green flowers, followed by berries in red, yellow, or orange, some edible. **SIZE (H × W):** Low growers, 3 feet x 6 feet; shrubs, 5 to 20 feet x as wide. **SUN:** Full sun. **MULCH:** Rock, gravel, shredded or chipped bark. **LANDSCAPE USE:** Low growers for groundcovers and slope stabilizers; small shrubs planted in drifts on hillsides or in borders; plant larger types along drives or as background. Some spread by suckers. No pruning for evergreens; prune deciduous suckering types to four buds. Deep, infrequent watering till established, then no water.

# Viburnum

*Viburnum* spp.

**ZONES:** 2–10. Viburnum are evergreen and deciduous shrubs growing in woodlands and thickets of Asia and North and South America. Their leaves vary widely from deep green oval and rounded, *fleshy, toothed, serrated*, or *deeply lobed* with deciduous species showing brilliant fall foliage in orange, red, and yellow. They all bloom from spring to summer in white, pink, and red flower clusters, some scented, and form berries in pink, red, or blue-black. **SIZE (H × W):** Many from compact 5 feet x as wide as 15 feet x 12 feet. **SUN:** Full sun. **MULCH:** Chipped or shredded bark. **LANDSCAPE USE:** Use viburnum as a natural hedge, in drifts along a drive, in groups in the midground, or large types for screening. Evergreen viburnum make good container plants. Prune only for errant branches; allow space for natural growth. Water deeply and infrequently after establishment.

# Agave

*Agave* spp.

**ZONES:** 6–11. Agave bask in the desert heat and warm mountainous regions of Mexico and southwestern U.S. The leaves are *elongated, narrow* to *slightly rounded, elliptical* and *fleshy*. Most have *spiny edges and tips. Gray-green, blue-gray, light green* to *green edged in red, black, yellow,* or *white* leaves form rosettes. When mature, seven to ten years, agave send out 6- to 20-foot flower spikes, resembling large asparagus stalks. The long-lasting, yellow, funnel-shaped blooms open for show-stopping drama until black seeds form. The parent rosette dies, but pups take its place. **SIZE (H × W):** 1 to 5 feet x 1 to 5 feet. **SUN:** Full sun to part shade. **MULCH:** Gravel, stone, sand. **LANDSCAPE USE:** Use as a focal point or in containers, planted in masses or sweeps on slopes. Slow-grower. Occasional deep watering in the heat of summer.

# Echeveria

*Echeveria* spp.

**ZONES:** 5–10. Echeveria are native to desert climates in Mexico, growing in rocky, sandy locations. Round, *plump, fleshy,* smooth, sometimes *hairy leaves* in *light green, white-green, lime-green,* and combinations edged in red that form tight clumps of rosettes. Blooms, on succulent stems held above the foliage, are bell-shaped clusters in pink, red, yellow, or orange in summer. **SIZE (H × W):** 2 to 24 inches x 4 to 36 inches, depending upon species and hybrid. **SUN:** Full sun. **MULCH:** Rock, sand, gravel. **LANDSCAPE USE:** Use singly in shallow containers, in rock and succulent gardens, in drifts along dry streambeds, or in groupings in the borders. Many hybrids in various sizes and brilliant leaf colors. In hottest summer climes, grow in part shade. Occasional deep waterings in summer.

# Hens n' Chicks

*Sempervivium* spp.

**ZONES:** 4–10. Hens n' chicks grow naturally in mountainous regions of Asia and Europe. Depending upon the species and its many hybrids, it has rosettes of *thick, fleshy* leaves—some with spines on the tips, others with *hairy* or *waxy* coatings. Light green, *gray* to *white,* burgundy-tipped, or deep burgundy to black foliage, flowers are not as showy as the foliage, but come in summer in yellow, white, pink, or red. **SIZE (H × W):** 8 to 12 inches x 1 to 2 feet, forming a dense mat. **SUN:** Full sun. **MULCH:** Stone, rock, sand. **LANDSCAPE USE:** Use in rock gardens, en masse as groundcover, in the front of succulent borders, in sweeps in desert gardens, and in containers. Water deeply when leaves start to shrivel; no fertilizer.

# Iceplant

*Lampranthus* spp.

**ZONES:** 8–13. Iceplant is native to South Africa, growing naturally on the coast in hot, semi-desert locations. It is a prostrate, lower growing succulent with small, three-sided *fleshy* leaves in green or *gray-green*. Daisylike flowers are profuse and blanket the sprawling plant from winter to spring in pink, red, yellow, or purple. **SIZE (H × W):** 12 to 20 inches x indefinite spread. **SUN:** Full sun. **MULCH:** Rock, gravel, sand. **LANDSCAPE USE:** Use iceplant to cover slopes, in sweeps along drives, in rock gardens, in containers, in color borders; in colder areas use as a long-blooming spring, summer annual. Available as 2-, 4-, or 6-inch plants in flats. Deadhead or cut back after blooming to encourage new soft growth; stems become woody with age. Water to establish, then minimal watering; water-soluble fertilizer, monthly in containers.

# Stonecrop

*Sedum* spp.

**ZONES:** 3–10. Stonecrop grows naturally in a broad range of climates in Europe, Africa, Japan, Korea, the British Isles, and the Mediterranean. They are quite varied in leaf and form by habitats. *Tiny*, elliptical, round, large, *ruffled, smooth, shiny, slightly toothed, succulent*, green, *light green, yellow-, blue-,* and *gray-green* leaves cluster densely in rosettes or along fleshy stems. Stonecrop is clumping, spreading, upright, or open-branching, depending upon type. Flowers are small, star-shaped in clusters late summer through fall in yellow, pink, white, red, salmon, and purple. **SIZE (H × W):** 2 inches to 5 feet x 1 to 3 feet. **SUN:** Full sun to part shade. **MULCH:** Rock, gravel, shredded or chipped bark. **LANDSCAPE USE:** Use in rock and succulent gardens, as groundcover, in color borders, in drifts along dry streambeds, on slopes, and in containers. Minimal watering.

# Yucca

*Yucca* spp.

**ZONES:** 5–10. Yucca grows naturally in hot, dry desert climates, open plains, and dunes in the southwestern and southeastern portions of the U.S., and Mexico and Central America. Grown for their foliage, long, *lancelike*, green and *green variegated with yellow or white edges or stripes* and their dramatic flower spikes in white, forming from summer to autumn. Forming evergreen clumps in a tight or loose V-shape, yucca makes a dramatic focal point. **SIZE (H × W):** 3 to 30 feet tall x 3 to 10 feet wide. **SUN:** Full sun. **MULCH:** Gravel, rock, sand. **LANDSCAPE USE:** Use in succulent- or desertscapes as a background screen, plant in groups or drifts or as an accent in a large pot in container gardens. Some used as trees. Deadhead spent flower spikes. Keep soil dry or deep, regular watering, depending upon species.

# Ash

*Fraxinus* spp.

**ZONES:** 4–10. Mostly deciduous, ash trees are native to the eastern and southwestern U.S., Mexico, and Europe, growing naturally in woodlands, tolerant of dry, windy, hot, cold, and any soil conditions. They are grown for their classic shade tree form and their foliage, which is *linear*, sometimes *serrated, leathery*, in light or mid-green, turning golden yellow, red, orange, purple in fall, depending upon the type. Irregular, deep watering in summer. **SIZE (H × W):** 18 to 80 feet x 10 to 60 feet. **SUN:** Full sun. **MULCH:** Shredded or chipped bark. **LANDSCAPE USE:** Use ash in groves at property edges, along drives, as a focal point or accent. Some species litter, but many cultivars are available that are much cleaner; choose to fit your space. Prune for crossing branches when young, keep open crown at maturity for wind to pass.

# Catalpa

*Catalpa* spp.

**ZONES:** 4–9. Catalpa is deciduous, growing along sunny streambeds and forest edges in central and southeastern U.S. Grown for its foliage: large, *glossy or fuzzy undersides*, mid- to deep green, *heart-shaped*, or *deeply veined*; for clusters of 2-inch trumpet-shaped, tropical-looking flowers in white with brown or yellow markings; and large, attractive, reddish-brown seedpods dripping from a beautifully structured canopy in late autumn. **SIZE (H × W):** 30 to 50 feet tall x as wide (species). **SUN:** Full sun. **MULCH:** Chipped or shredded bark. **LANDSCAPE USE:** Grow as a focal point, with mulch in its understory to avoid concern about dropped leaves and pods. *C. bignonoides* leaves are odoriferous; *C. speciosa* are not. There are cultivars with yellow-green or purplish green leaves, some smaller to just 6 feet tall and wide. Prune to shape and to lift canopy when young. Deep, infrequent watering, none in winter.

# Chinese Flame Tree

*Koelrueteria* spp.

**ZONES:** 5–10. Chinese flame tree grows naturally in dry woodlands in China, Korea, and Taiwan. One of two species in the genus, golden rain tree is similar in characteristics, the variable being the number of leaflets on the stem. Both have *divided leaves* of oval leaflets that may be slightly *toothed*, showing brief fall foliage in golden yellow. Early, mid-, to late summer blooms are yellow clusters leading to showy seed capsules in pink to red or brown that persist on the tree. **SIZE (H × W):** 20 to 40 feet x 25 to 40 feet. **SUN:** Full sun. **MULCH:** Chipped or shredded bark. **LANDSCAPE USE:** Use as specimen trees, focal points, in open areas for shade, as patio or lawn trees. Prune to maintain high, open canopy. Water deeply, infrequently to establish; then occasional deep watering in summer.

# Chinese Pistache

*Pistacia chinensis*

**ZONES:** 5–9. Chinese pistache is native to western China, growing in dry habitats. Deciduous, it has *deeply divided*, dark green, *shiny, toothed, leathery leaflets*. Flowers appear in mid- to late spring in red to green clusters, forming small berries (unlike *P. vera*) in red, turning turquoise blue on female trees. Fall foliage turns brilliant yellow, orange, and red. **SIZE (H × W):** 50 to 80 feet x 20 to 30 feet. **SUN:** Full sun. **MULCH:** Shredded or chipped bark. **LANDSCAPE USE:** Use Chinese pistache to line drives, as focal points, at meadow edges. Chinese pistache grows in all conditions; may be considered invasive. If it's not available in local nurseries, then avoid buying from mail-order or from outside your area. Prune young trees to train for structure. Water deeply, infrequently until established, then deeply only in long droughts.

# Cypress

*Cupressus* spp.

**ZONES:** 6–10. Cypress are evergreen conifers, native to dry hillsides in coastal California, southern and southwestern U.S., Tibet, and Kashmir. They have flattened, *scalelike*, green, *silver-green, blue-green*, or golden yellow leaves, some *aromatic*, growing densely on sometimes pendulous branches, with reddish-brown trunks, which turn scaly or smooth with age. Small, 1- to 2-inch-diameter cones remain on the tree. Growth habits from classic conical to wide crown. **SIZE (H × W):** 10 to 60 feet x 5 to 20 feet, depending upon species. **SUN:** Full sun. **MULCH:** Chipped or shredded bark. **LANDSCAPE USE:** Use smaller types as hedgerows or in containers (*C.* 'Tiny Tower'), larger forms as specimen trees (*C. cashmeriana*) or in clusters for groves lining drives or for windbreaks (*C. arizonica, C. forbesii*). Grow established plants from containers. No pruning. Water deeply, infrequently until established, then only in extended drought.

# Desert Willow

*Chilopsis linearis*

**ZONES:** 6–11. Desert willow, native to the southwestern U.S., grows in low desert washes to high desert (5,000 feet). One species in its genus, but many cultivars have been developed for evergreen or sterile selections (no seedpods). Deciduous, it has green, *linear, narrow* leaves that curve slightly, with large, scented, trumpetlike blooms from spring to fall in pink, white, lilac, purple, red, and lavender. After bloom, trees hold onto the seedpods through winter. With maturity, the trunk becomes attractive with gnarled and shaggy branches. **SIZE (H × W):** 15 to 30 feet tall and wide. **SUN:** Full sun. **MULCH:** Gravel, stone, shredded or chipped bark. **LANDSCAPE USE:** Use as focal points, in drifts to line drives or surround gardens, in groups with understory plantings, and in small gardens. Prune only to show off form. Regular, deep watering to establish, then infrequently in summer.

# Hackberry

*Celtis* spp.

**ZONES:** 2–9. Hackberry trees grow naturally in habitats ranging from streambeds to dry, rocky hillsides in the southwestern U.S., Pacific Northwest, China, Korea, and the Mediterranean. Deciduous hackberry has deep green, *toothed* leaves that show yellow fall foliage, forming a rounded crown with slightly pendulous branching. Inconspicuous green flowers in spring are followed by small orange-red berries that turn to black, beloved by foragers and birds. **SIZE (H × W):** 18 to 40 feet x 20 to 50 feet. **SUN:** Full sun to part shade. **MULCH:** Chipped or shredded bark. **LANDSCAPE USE:** Use fast-growing hackberry for quick shade as a lawn tree, next to the home (deep rooting, does not lift sidewalks), as a grove along drives. Hackberries have some fire resistance, tolerating wind and heat. No pruning. Water deeply, infrequently to establish, then only in extended drought.

# Incense Cedar

*Calocedrus decurrens*

**ZONES:** 5–8. Incense cedar comes from dry, warm, temperate forests and mountains from Oregon to Baja California. It is an evergreen conifer, with small yellow to brown cones and bright green, *scalelike, flattened* foliage that densely covers the reddish-brown trunk. In the heat of summer, its pungent scent wafts in the breeze. **SIZE (H × W):** 90 feet x 15 feet. **SUN:** Full sun to part shade. **MULCH:** Shredded or chipped bark. **LANDSCAPE USE:** Use the stately, very tall, but narrow tree as a focal point, in groupings for a dense windbreak, in drifts to line drives. Slow-growing the first couple of years; plant a 5-gallon or 15-gallon container for starting size; once established it grows 2 feet yearly. Conifers need no pruning. Deep, infrequent watering just during establishment, then only during extended drought.

# Juniper

*Juniperus* spp.

**ZONES:** 2–10. Juniper, an evergreen conifer, comes from a large genus of over 60 members with as many cultivars. Native from dry forests to rocky hillsides throughout North America, they have juvenile *needlelike foliage*, softening to *scalelike* and *flattened* with maturity in green, *gray-green*, and golden yellow. Very small cones; female plants produce edible fruit that persist on trees until ripe, when they shower the ground in bluish-purple berries. **SIZE (H × W):** 2 to 50 feet x 2 to 60 feet, depending upon type. **SUN:** Full sun to part shade. **MULCH:** Shredded and chipped bark. **LANDSCAPE USE:** Small types are used for groundcovers and shrubs; taller, stately types as focal points, in drifts for hedgerows, windbreaks, and screens; cluster in groups for groves and accents. Use smaller cultivars in containers. No pruning. Deep, regular watering to establish, then only in extended drought.

# Maidenhair Tree

*Ginkgo biloba*

**ZONES:** 3–9. Maidenhair tree is an ancient species that lived with dinosaurs and grew worldwide. Now, the only remaining native stands grow in China. It is a slow-growing deciduous tree, with *lobed, fanlike foliage* in light green that turns beautiful golden yellow in autumn; leaves remain on the tree until they simultaneously fall, creating a golden carpet beneath. **SIZE (H × W):** 35 to 50 feet x 25 to 40 feet at maturity. **SUN:** Full sun. **MULCH:** Shredded or chipped bark. **LANDSCAPE USE:** Tolerant of any conditions, use ginkgo in groves, as lawn specimen trees, along drives, as focal points. A few cultivars are available, but only male plants are sold commercially. Prune only branches that are awkward to the structure when immature, then no pruning. Water deeply and infrequently until 20 feet tall, then only occasional deep watering in summer.

# Maple

*Acer* spp.

**ZONES:** 2–9. Maples are native to woodlands in North and Central America, Asia, North Africa, and Europe. Mostly deciduous, there are a few evergreens, long-living to 100 years. Leaves are oval to *deeply divided* and *palmate*, deep green, red, burgundy, and may have *white* or *lighter undersides*, some *variegated* green and white. In cold regions, beautiful fall colors appear in red, orange, golden yellow, and combinations. Inconspicuous flowers, showy winged fruits follow. Give maple trees room to grow to their mature size. **SIZE (H × W):** 15 to 70 feet x as wide. **SUN:** Full sun to part shade. **MULCH:** Leaves, chipped bark. **LANDSCAPE USE:** Use for shade as focal points, plant in groves in large open areas, smaller types in containers or sited in the understories of larger trees. Prune to train scaffold branches. Water deeply and regularly; no water in winter.

# Mazari Palm

*Nannorrhops ritchiana*

**ZONES:** 7–11. Mazari palm is native to southwestern Asia, growing in sandy dunes where summers are hot and dry. Known for extreme toughness, mazari palm is able to survive any amount of heat (as long as it is dry), high winds, and cold snaps where temperatures have been reported below -20 degrees Fahrenheit. A clumping evergreen, with large, 4-foot-diameter *fanlike fronds* in *silver-gray* or *blue-green* on spineless stems. **SIZE (H × W):** 10 to 20 feet x slightly wider. **SUN:** Full sun. **MULCH:** Stone, gravel, sand. **LANDSCAPE USE:** Single or multi-trunked, use mazari palm in groups as background plants, singly as clumping focal points, or in drifts along dry streambeds. Grows slowly. Cut off browned fronds to keep it clean. Water infrequently but deeply to establish, then allow to go dry; needs well-draining soil.

# Mediterranean Fan Palm

*Chamaerops humilis*

**ZONES:** 8–11. Mediterranean fan palm is the only palm native to Europe, growing naturally on dry, sandy, and rocky slopes in western Mediterranean and northwestern Africa. It is among the cold-hardiest of palms, a short, clumping type with *blue-green* fronds on stalks covered in *spines*. Slow growing, it has been known to survive to 0 degrees Fahrenheit (for short periods), can take an occasional frost, and tolerates wind and heat. **SIZE (H × W):** 20 feet x as wide at maturity. **SUN:** Full sun to part shade. **MULCH:** Gravel, stone, chipped or shredded bark. **LANDSCAPE USE:** Use in containers, in groupings by pools or water features, in drifts along drives, or in the understories of other trees. Cut off browned older fronds at their base. Water infrequently and deeply to establish, then deeply a few times during summer.

# Mimosa

*Albizia julibrissin*

**ZONES:** 6–10. Mimosa trees grow naturally in lean, poor, arid soils in Africa, Asia, and Australia in open sites. Deciduous, semi-deciduous in warmer climates, it has *finely divided, feathery yellow-green* leaves followed by fluffy, silky, soft to hot pink flowers in summer. Mimosas are short-lived, spanning 25 to 40 years, with broad canopies up to twice the tree's height. **SIZE (H × W):** 40 feet x 80 feet. **SUN:** Full sun. **MULCH:** Chipped or shredded bark. **LANDSCAPE USE:** Use as focal points on a lower terrace so it can be viewed from above or as small patio trees if you don't mind flowers blanketing everything. Mulch its understory for no worries about leaf and flower drop. Can be invasive. Start with 1- or 5-gallon containers; prune off suckers. Water deeply, infrequently for faster growth, none in winter.

# Oak

*Quercus* spp.

**ZONES:** 3–10. Oaks are long-lived, stately, deciduous, semi-deciduous, or evergreen trees that grow in scrubby outbacks and woodlands throughout the northern hemisphere. Their deep to medium green leaves are *small, serrated, leathery, shiny,* large, *deeply divided, palmate, curved,* or *lance-shaped.* Deciduous types have brilliant orange, red, and burgundy fall foliage. **SIZE (H × W):** 20 to 60 feet x as wide. **SUN:** Full sun to part shade. **MULCH:** Chipped or shredded bark, oak leaves. **LANDSCAPE USE:** Plant single types as specimen trees, focal points, or groves. Most are slow-growers. No pruning is best. Plant non-rootbound, 1- or 5-gallon oaks in spring in cold winter areas; otherwise, in fall, hire an arborist to plant boxed trees. Use mycorrhizal organics in backfill. Deep, regular watering applied to 1 foot using drip or soaker hose at outer edges of rootball, once a week during its first summer. Avoid watering trunks.

# Pine

*Pinus* spp.

**ZONES:** 3–10. Pines grow naturally in forests in high mountain regions to low desert areas worldwide. They are a huge genus, with a pine suitable, hardy, and tolerant of almost every situation: wind, heat, drought, cold, and variable soils. Pines have bundles of 2 to 5 *needles* and cones from 1 inch to over 14 inches long. Some have classic conical shapes, some wide crowns and branches, drooping to the ground. **SIZE (H × W):** 3 to 80 feet x 2 to 30 feet, depending upon type. **SUN:** Full sun. **MULCH:** Pine needles, chipped or shredded bark. **LANDSCAPE USE:** Use single pines as focal points, lawn trees, or a background for perennial beds, plant in groups for a natural stand, in drifts for windbreaks or screens, or to line property perimeters. No pruning. Water deeply and infrequently to establish, then only in extended drought.

# Purple Leaf Plum

*Prunus cerasifera*

**ZONES:** 5–9. Purple leaf plum (non-fruiting) is native to rocky slopes, sandy, and scrub locations in South America and Southeast Asia. Purple leaf plum is grown for its foliage, oval, *slightly serrated* and reddish purple until fall, when it drops it leaves. In early spring, buds bring forth bowl-shaped blooms, some fragrant, in white and cultivars in pale to bright pink to red. **SIZE (H × W):** 10 to 30 feet x as wide depending on cultivar. **SUN:** Full sun. **MULCH:** Chipped or shredded bark. **LANDSCAPE USE:** Purple leaf plum is a good patio, lawn, or street tree; plant as single focal points or along drives. They are not particularly messy, easy-care, have an open-branching upright scaffold, and live about 20 years. Prune off suckers. Water deeply, infrequently to establish, then only a couple of deep soaks during summer.

# Redbud

*Cercis* spp.

**ZONES:** 4–9. Redbuds grow naturally from woodlands to rocky hillsides in eastern U.S., California, Utah, Arizona, China, and Japan. Deciduous redbuds are popular for beautiful, brightly colored pealike blooms that cover the tree in early spring before leaves form. Occasional multibranching makes redbud useful as a shrub. Broad, *heart-shaped*, green to *blue-green, shiny* foliage turns yellow or red in autumn. In early spring, colorful red buds begin the floral show, opening in clusters of rosy pink, white, deep purple, or lavender-pink blooms, followed by flattened pods, remaining through winter. **SIZE (H × W):** 3 to 15 feet x as wide. **SUN:** Full sun to part shade. **MULCH:** Chipped or shredded bark. **LANDSCAPE USE:** Use as focal points, in large containers, along fencelines, in clusters in perennial gardens. Prune young trees to a single trunk; otherwise, prune only crossing branches. Deep, infrequent watering, none in winter.

# Asparagus

*Asparagus officinalis*

**ZONES:** 3–8. Asparagus is a hardy, long-living perennial, native to the Mediterranean, growing in sandy or coastal locations. Deciduous, it grows from tuberous roots, first sending up leafless stalks (the third season) in early spring. Edible spears continue throughout spring into summer, when small, insignificant flowers form on tall stems *lined with spines. Fine feathery* foliage turns golden yellow in fall. **SIZE (H × W):** Stems 3 feet x clumping to 4 feet. **SUN:** Full sun. **MULCH:** Straw. **LANDSCAPE USE:** Use in back of flower borders, in drifts in perennial beds, in blocks in vegetable gardens (where it can naturalize). Leave foliage until the following spring, removing when you see spears arising from the base. Deep, regular watering twice weekly its first season; thereafter, deep watering weekly if no rain, no winter watering. Top-dress with compost at end of each growing season.

# Citrus

*Citrus* spp.

**ZONES:** 8–10. Citrus grows naturally in scrubby outbacks, thickets, and forest edges in Southeast Asia. Many being grafted and cultivars, evergreen citrus sometimes have *spiny trunks* or stems; *shiny* oval leaves; white, scented blossoms in spring, leading to fruit from spring through (mild) winter. Some are more cold-hardy than others, but all need heat to produce. **SIZE (H × W):** 5 to 20 feet x 5 to 30 feet. **SUN:** Full sun. **MULCH:** Organic compost, shredded or chipped bark, stone. **LANDSCAPE USE:** Use citrus trees as focal points, in groves, as street trees, background plants in edible gardens, and dwarf types in containers and in greenhouses. Prune freeze-damaged branches in late spring, summer. Water deeply to 2 feet, twice weekly its first season; then every two weeks if no rain. Fertilize with nitrogen, per recommendations.

# Currants

*Ribes* spp.

**ZONES:** 2–10. Currants, deciduous shrubs, are native to scrub and rocky locations in South America, Europe, coastal California to Baja, and central U.S. They have *deeply lobed, toothed* or *scalloped* green leaves, some with golden fall foliage. Small, scented, bright yellow, white, or pink flowers cover branches in spring, followed by red turning to black berries in summer to fall. *Ribes* include currants (no spines) and gooseberries (spines). This genus can host white pine blister rust, so look for resistant types. **SIZE (H × W):** 3 to 12 feet x as wide. **SUN:** Full sun to part shade. **MULCH:** Shredded or chipped bark. **LANDSCAPE USE:** Use singly for focal points or as background hedgerows or screens. No pruning except cut older woody and non-producing canes to 4 inches so new branches form. Water deeply, frequently to establish, then only in drought. No fertilizer.

# Garden Sage

*Salvia officinalis*

**ZONES:** 4–11. Garden sage grows naturally in the Mediterranean and North Africa, thriving in meadows, rocky outcrops, and woodland edges. Evergreen, perennial garden sage has long, *aromatic, gray-green* to *variegated leaves* with *lighter undersides*, having *rough* or *slightly fuzzy leaf surfaces*. **SIZE (H × W):** 12 to 36 inches x 24 to 36 inches. **SUN:** Full sun to part shade. **MULCH:** Chipped or shredded bark. **LANDSCAPE USE:** Use sage singly in container edible gardens or rock gardens, in masses for groundcover, in sweeps in perennial beds, or in groups in color borders. Many cultivars. Prune leggy plants to 3 inches in early spring to encourage new bushy growth. Replace woody plants every four years or so. Cut new, soft growth for fresh use or dry for storage. Water deeply, infrequently; no water in cold winters. No fertilizer.

# Garlic

*Allium sativum*

**ALL ZONES.** Garlic has been cultivated for thousands of years, its origin leading to China. It is a cool-season annual; plant seed (cloves) in fall for mature bulbs early to midsummer. In early spring, it sends up long, green, hollow stems. The green foliage turns yellow, dries, and collapses when it's time to harvest the edible bulb. **SIZE (H × W):** 18 inches x 2 inches. **SUN:** Full sun. **MULCH:** 4 inches of straw. **LANDSCAPE USE:** Plant singly in the landscape, in a space that has access for harvesting; leave in the ground for pest control around the base of fruit trees and between tomato plants, or in designated garden space and plant warm-season crops after harvest. Water deeply, regularly for a month after planting, then no water until stems pop up in spring. Water deeply, regularly until tops turn brown, stop watering till harvest. Incorporate compost before planting.

# Grapes

*Vitis* spp.

**ZONES:** 5–10. Grapes grow naturally in thickets, woodlands, and along dry riverbeds in China, Korea, and Japan. A deciduous vine (some are sprawling shrubs), grapes have large, *deeply lobed* or *toothed* leaves growing on twisted branches, with *peeling bark* in maturity. Stems twine and tiny insignificant flowers form on strong tendrils that hold clusters of fruits, appearing late summer to fall. Fall foliage is golden yellow, turning orange, red, or brown. **SIZE (H × W):** Unchecked, they climb to 50 feet, but follow pruning guides that come with the bare-root or container varieties for size and production desired. **SUN:** Full sun. **MULCH:** Grass or meadow clippings, straw. **LANDSCAPE USE:** Use table grapes to climb an arbor, a fence, or a trellis or grow varietals in vineyards. Water deeply, twice weekly in spring; stop watering when fruit sets. Low nutrient demands; fertilize by soil sample recommendations.

# Melons

*Cucumis melo*

**ALL ZONES.** Melons are native to central Asia, Africa, and the Middle East, basking in their arid heat. They are a warm-season annual, growing on long vining stems with large tropical leaves, flowering and fruiting 65 to 90 days from planting. **SIZE (H × W):** 6 to 12 inches x 3 to 6 feet. **SUN:** Full sun. **MULCH:** Straw. **LANDSCAPE USE:** Grow melons as groundcover, on a trellis or fence with slings to hold the heavy fruits, along dry streambeds in landscapes, compact types in containers. In a designated garden bed, interplant with corn, radishes, sunflower, or nasturtium. Sow seed a foot apart in late spring or early summer or plant seedlings or plants if gardening in short-season areas. Water deeply but infrequently; avoid watering on the foliage and allow the soil to dry out between waterings. Incorporate compost before planting.

# Pomegranate

*Punica granatum*

**ZONES:** 6–10. Pomegranates are native to southeastern Europe to the Himalayas, growing in scrubby outback regions. Multibranching, they can be used as a shrub or trained into a small tree. Deciduous, *small*, oval, *glossy*, bronze turning green leaves grow densely on strong stems. In colder climates, pomegranate gives golden yellow fall foliage. Red blooms in spring turn to shiny, red, baseball-sized fruits by fall. When completely red, the hard shell is cracked open, revealing mature sweet seeds and pulp. **SIZE (H × W):** 15 to 20 feet x as wide. **SUN:** Full sun. **MULCH:** Shredded and chipped bark. **LANDSCAPE USE:** Use pomegranate as a focal point, as green screens, background shrubs, and dwarf types in containers. Many cultivars. Prune young trees to tree forms; otherwise no pruning. Water deeply, infrequently spring to fall, then no winter watering. No fertilizer.

# Thyme

*Thymus* spp.

**ZONES:** 4–10. Thyme is a semi-evergreen to evergreen perennial, native to dry grasslands in the Mediterranean, Europe, and Asia. *High in oils*, this herb has *tiny*, green, *gray-green*, or *variegated leaves*, covering sprawling or upright stems. **SIZE (H × W):** 2 to 12 inch tall x 12 to 36 inch wide. **SUN:** Full sun to part shade. **MULCH:** Chipped or shredded bark mulch to establish; then let it take its course. **LANDSCAPE USE:** Many types; low, groundhuggers spread a little for filler between pavers, in rock gardens; wider spreading for lawn alternative or plant on slopes. Use taller, bushier forms in containers, in masses in perennial borders, in sweeps under deciduous trees. Prune to encourage new, soft growth in fall in warm-winter climates and early spring in colder areas. Water deeply, infrequently; shorter types need water through summer, taller need infrequent water after first season. No fertilizer.

# Photo credits

**Andre Viette**: 141 (middle)

**Bill Adams**: 143 (middle)

**Charles Mann**: Cover, 22, 27, 150 (top)

**Conservation Garden Park, West Jordan, Utah**: 32 (all), 33 (both), 38 (top), 78, 104, 108 (all), 128 (left)

**Deneen Powell Atelier, Inc. (DPA), San Diego, California**: 3, 37, 39, 42, 43, 49, 54, 58

**Desert Springs Preserve, Las Vegas, Nevada**: 36 (right)

**Diana Maranhao**: 5 (right, top and bottom), 6, 8, 15 (both), 17 (right), 38 (bottom), 44, 48 (both), 55, 66, 73, 77, 82, 83, 85, 91 (bottom), 93 (right), 94 (right), 95, 96 (bottom), 98, 105, 116, 117, 118, 119 (left), 121, 123, 124, 125, 128 (right), 129, 130 (all), 134 (middle), 148 (middle), 154 (bottom), 160 (top), 161 (top, bottom), 164 (bottom)

**Helen M. Stone, Southwest Trees & Turf**: 42

**Hunter Industries**: 62, 69

**JC Raulston Arboretum at NC State University**: 159 (middle),

**Jerry Pavia**: 132 (top), 139 (top), 145 (bottom) 146 (bottom), 150 (bottom), 151 (top, middle), 152 (bottom), 156 (top), 157 (middle), 163 (bottom), 166 (middle)

**John Cretti**: 147 (top)

**Judy Mielke**: 142 (bottom)

**Katie Elzer-Peters**: 89 (all), 120

**Lorenzo Gunn**: 162 (top)

**Loa LaDene, San Diego, California**: 36 (left)

**National Park Service; Lake Mead, Nevada**: 12 (bottom)

**Neil Soderstrom**: 160 (bottom)

**Netafim Irrigation**: 64, 72 (both), 73 (Ltd.)

**Prairie Nursery Inc.**: 20, 30, 31 (all), 65, 126

**Rain Bird Corporation, Drip Application Guide**: 68, 72

**Ruan Prange**: 28 (top right, bottom), 29

**Sandra Nyeholt**: 144 (bottom)

**Shutterstock**: spine, 1, 3, 8, 12 (top, both), 17 (left), 36 (left), 60, 81, 99, 113, 114, 119 (right), 122, 132 (middle), 133 (top, bottom), 134 (bottom), 136 (all), 137 (middle, bottom), 138 (all), 139 (middle), 140 (top, bottom), 142 (middle), 143 (bottom), 144 (top), 146 (top, middle), 147 (bottom), 149 (bottom), 153 (bottom), 155 (top, middle), 156 (middle, bottom), 157 (top), 158 (top), 159 (top), 160 (middle), 165 (middle, bottom), 166 (top)

**Stefani Trimmer**: 103

**Steve Harbour Landscapes**: 5 (bottom left), 18, 23 (all), 24 (all), 25 (all), 26 (all), 28 (top left), 34, 50 (both), 59, 86, 93 (left, both), 94 (left), 109, 110 (both), 112 (both)

**The Toro Company, Irrigation Division**: 74 (bottom right), 102

**The Water Conservation Garden, El Cajon, California**: 5 (top left), 63, 88 (both), 90, 91 (top), 100 (both), 103, 106, 107, 131

**Tom Eltzroth**: 132 (bottom), 133 (middle), 134 (top), 135 (all), 137 (top), 139 (bottom), 140 (middle), 141 (top, bottom), 142 (top), 143 (top), 144 (middle), 145 (top, middle), 147 (middle), 148 (top, bottom), 149 (top, middle), 150 (middle), 151 (bottom), 152 (top, middle), 153 (top, middle), 154 (top, middle), 155 (bottom), 157 (bottom), 158 (middle, bottom), 159 (bottom), 161 (middle), 162 (middle, bottom), 163 (top, middle), 164 (top, middle), 165 (top), 166 (bottom)

**West Coast Arborists, Inc.**: 37

# RESOURCES

## ASSOCIATIONS

Desert Green Foundation; www.desert-green.org

## EDUCATION

Colorado State Extension; CMG Garden Notes #212; The Living Soil; www.ext.colostate.edu/mg/gardennotes/212.html

Natural Resources Conservation Service/Soils; www.nrcs.usda.gov

University of Minnesota/Extension; www.extension.umn.edu

University of Nevada Cooperative Extension; www.unce.unr.edu

Texas A & M; Agrilife Extension; www.rainwaterharvesting.tamu.edu

Water Sense EPA Partnership Program; www.epa.gov/watersense

## IRRIGATION/DRAINAGE

Hunter Industries, Inc.; www.hunterindustries.com

NDS Pro; www.ndspro.com

Netafim USA; www.Netafimusa.com

Rain Bird Corporation; www.rainbird.com

Toro; www.toro.com/en-us/irrigation

## LANDSCAPE ARCHITECTURE/ GRAPHIC DESIGN

Immersive Experiential Learning: Deneen Powell Atelier, Inc.; San Diego, CA; www.dpadesign.com

## LANDSCAPE SERVICES

Falling Waters Landscape, Inc.; Owner: Ryan Prange; Encinitas, CA; www.fallingwaterslandscape.com

Steve Harbour Landscapes; Owner: Steve Harbour; San Diego, CA; www.steveharbourlandscapes.com

West Coast Arborists, Inc.; Owner: Rose Epperson; Anaheim, CA; www.westcoastarborists.com

## NURSERIES

High Country Gardens; www.highcountrygardens.com

Prairie Nursery, Inc.; Westfield, WI; www.prairienursery.com

## PUBLICATIONS

*A-Z Encyclopedia of Garden Plants;* by Christopher Brickell; The American Horticultural Society; DK Publishing; New York, NY; 1996

*Natural by Design;* by Judith Phillips; Museum of New Mexico Press; Sante Fe, NM; 1995

*Rainwater Harvesting; Vol. 1 & 2;* by Brad Lancaster; Rainsource Press; Tucson, AZ; 2006

*Soil Science & Management;* by Edward J. Plaster; Delmar Publishers, Inc.; Albany, NY; 1985

*Southwest Trees & Turf;* Editor: Helen M. Stone; www.swtreesandturf.com

*Teaming with Microbes;* by Jeff Lowenfels & Wayne Lewis; Timber Press, Inc.; Portland, OR; 2010

## WATER CONSERVATION/ SUSTAINABILITY DEMONSTRATION GARDENS

Conservation Garden Park; West Jordan, UT; www.conservationgardenpark.org

Denver Xeric Gardens; Denver Water; Denver, CO; www.denverwater.org/Conservation/Xeriscape/XeriscapeResources

Springs Preserve; Las Vegas, NV; www.springspreserve.org

The Water Conservation Garden; El Cajon, CA; www.thegarden.org

## INTERNET RESEARCH, STUDIES, INFORMATION

*A Guide to Estimating Irrigation Water Needs of Landscape Plantings in CA;* WUCOLS III; U of CA Extension; CA Dept. Of Water Resources; www.water.ca.gov/wateruseefficiency/docs/wucols00.pdf

U.S. Environmental Protection Agency; www.epa.gov

The Lawn Institute; www.thelawninstitute.org

*SERG Restoration Bulletin*; Soil Ecology & Restoration Group; David A. Bainbridge; www.sci.sdsu.edu/SERG

Native Plant Nurseries in Wisconsin; Wisconsin Dept of Natural Resources; www.dnr.wi.gov/files/PDF/pubs/ER/ER0698.pdf

U.S. Drought Monitor; www.drought.gov/drought/content/products-current-drought-and-monitoring-drought-indicators/us-drought-monitor

U.S. Geological Survey (USGS) Water Science School, Domestic Water Use; www.water.usgs.gov/edu/wudo.html

The Habitable Planet: Unit 8: Water Resources; www.learner.org/courses/envsci/unit/pdfs/unit8.pdf

University of California Agriculture: A Peer-Reviewed Article: Water-sorbing Polymers; www.californiaagriculture.ucanr.edu/landingpage.cfm?article=ca.v046n03p9&fulltext=yes

# GLOSSARY

**Acidic soil:** On a soil pH scale of 0 to 14, acidic soil has a pH reading of 6.0 or lower. Mildly acidic is 6.0 to 7.0.

**Aggregate:** Soil particles that are massed together.

**Alkaline soil:** On a soil pH scale of 0 to 14, alkaline soil has a pH higher than 7.0.

**Amendment:** Organic or inorganic material incorporated into the soil to improve it.

**Annual:** A plant that germinates (sprouts), flowers, and dies within one year.

**Aquifer:** An underground water-bearing formation.

**Backflow prevention device:** An irrigation system component that prevents water from going back into the potable water supply.

**Balled-and-burlapped (B&B):** Plants that have been grown in field rows, dug up with their soil intact, wrapped with burlap, and tied with twine.

**Balanced fertilizer:** A fertilizer with equal (or close to it) amounts of the three main plant nutrients—nitrogen, phosphorus, and potassium.

**Bareroot:** Plants that are shipped dormant, without being planted in a container or having soil around their roots.

**Beneficial insects:** Insects that perform valuable services such as pollination and pest control. Examples: ladybugs, spiders, and bees.

**Berm and Basin:** A berm is mounded soil that stops the flow of water, capturing it in a basin that holds the water until it can be absorbed into the soil.

**Bulb:** Swollen underground storage organs with small, living plants already growing inside. Examples: tulips, daffodils, and hyacinths.

**Canopy:** The overhead branching area of a tree, including foliage.

**Colonize:** When plants spread or grow in a new area other than their native habitat.

**Compost:** The resulting material after decomposition of organic matter.

**Conifer:** A plant that produces cones. Most are needled evergreens, such as spruce, pine, and fir.

**Container:** Any pot or vessel that is used for growing plants.

**Cool-season plant:** A flowering plant that thrives in cooler weather.

**Corm:** A fat, flat, scaly underground stem that's planted underground similar to a bulb. Leaves and flowers emerge from nodes on the corm. Examples: crocus, gladiolus, freesia.

**Cultivar:** A plant that has been bred or selected for having one or more distinct traits from the species, then given a name to set it apart, such as 'Pardon Me,' a cultivar of daylily.

**Crown:** The branch work that makes up a tree canopy

**Dappled:** Refers to open or light shade created by high tree branches or tree foliage in which patches of sunlight and shade intermingle.

**Deadhead:** To remove dead flowers in order to encourage further bloom, neaten the plant, and prevent the plant from self-sowing.

**Deciduous:** A plant that loses its leaves seasonally, typically in fall or early winter; some native plants in summer.

**Decomposed granite:** A soil type that has been formed from parent granite material. Also processed and used for permeable paths, roads.

**Desiccate:** When leaves completely dry up.

**Diversion swale:** A low-lying depression in the soil used to direct the flow of water to another location.

**Divide:** The process of digging up bulbs and clumping perennials, separating the roots, and replanting the pieces.

**Drought tolerant:** A plant's ability to survive and tolerate periods of drought.

**Dormancy:** The period when plants stop growing in order to conserve energy, in winter, summer in the case of some native plants and cool-season perennials, and spring-blooming bulbs.

**Drainage line:** Corrugated or perforated pipe that moves water underground to another location.

**Drip irrigation:** The slow release of water delivered through tubing and emitters. Also called micro-irrigation.

**Drip line:** Refers to the outermost reaches of the branches of a tree.

**Dwarf:** Describes a plant whose size is less than that of the species' standard or usual size.

**Earthworks:** When contours, hills, berms, basins, ponds, or other landscape features are constructed using soil and rock as the primary components.

**Emitter:** A drip irrigation component that delivers water to plants, measured in gallons of water emitted per hour (gph).

**Evergreen:** A plant that keeps its leaves year-round, instead of dropping them seasonally. These can be needled plants as well as broad-leaf ones.

**Established plant:** Refers to the stage when a plant reaches maturity and exhibits continued healthy growth. Varies with the type of plant. Perennials are established after two or three seasons, trees after five or more years.

**Flats:** Trays that hold smaller pots and cell packs.

**Full sun:** Areas of the garden that receive direct sunlight for at least six to eight hours a day.

**Germination:** The process by which a plant emerges from a seed or a spore.

**Grafted:** A plant that has two parts—a lower section with strong roots and a top part (the "scion") that has been attached for a desired growth habit, such as dwarf size, disease resistance, or improved flowering or fruiting.

**Granular fertilizer:** A type of fertilizer that comes in a dry, pellet-like form.

**Green screen/wall:** A screen or wall made of plants grouped closely together.

**Hardiness zone:** A numeral system developed by the U.S. Department of Agriculture to designate an area's average annual low temperature. Plants are then given ratings according to the temperatures they'll survive.

**Hardscape:** Features in the landscape other than plants (softscape), such as benches, fences, sidewalks, etc.

**Head:** A spray irrigation component that delivers water to plants, measured in gallons per minute (gpm).

**Hybrid:** A plant produced by crossing two genetically different plants, usually to achieve a desired trait, new color, or some other perceived improvement.

**Insecticide:** A compound used to kill or control insects.

**Interplant:** When two or more different types of plants are planted together in the same landscape bed so they share resources.

**Invasive:** Refers to a plant that multiplies by self-sowing seed or by self-dividing to the extent that it threatens growth of other plants.

**Irrigation timer:** A clock that automatically activates valves to water the landscape.

**Manifold:** A section of an irrigation system that may contain a pressure regulator, valve, backflow prevention device, and filter. For rainwater catchment systems, also a pump.

**Microbe:** A microscopic organism, in this case living in the soil.

**Microclimate:** Small sections of a property that deviate slightly from the prevailing, surrounding climate. A courtyard with stone walls, for example, likely will have warmer, less windy conditions than the rest of a yard.

**Mulch:** Any type of material that is spread over the soil surface, generally to suppress weeds and retain soil moisture.

**Mycorrhizae:** Fungi that collect around roots, forming a beneficial relationship that enhances root growth.

**Native plant:** In terms of U.S. native plants, these are species that were growing here before the arrival of European settlers.

**Native soil:** The soil that we have in our landscape before it has been amended. The soil in which native plants grow in their natural habitat.

**Naturalize:** When plants adapt, grow, and spread as though native to the area.

**Organic:** Any carbon-based material capable of decomposition and decay. Here it refers to a fertilizer, mulch, soil amendment, or product derived from naturally occurring materials instead of synthesized in a lab or factory.

**Ornamental:** Refers to any plant favored for its ornamental characteristics, flower, leaf, structure, rather than for producing edible fruit, vegetable, or foliage.

**Packs:** Multi-compartment containers, usually made out of thin plastic and used to sell small plants. They're most often used for annual flowers and vegetables and come in 3-, 4-, and 6-packs.

**Part sun/part shade:** Areas of the garden that get direct sunlight for part of the day (less than six hours) and that are in shade for part of the day (at least three hours of sunlight at some point).

**Perennial:** A plant that lives for more than two years. Usually used to describe herbaceous plants.

**Permeable:** A surface or material that allows water to pass through it.

**pH:** A figure designating the acidity or the alkalinity of soil as measured on a scale of 0 to 14, with 7.0 being neutral.

**Pinch:** The process of removing top or side growth on a plant to direct the growth.

**Plug:** A portion of a plant that has roots, allowing it to be planted to grow into a mature plant. Often used to plant a lawn.

**Pollard:** A specialized form of pruning that begins when trees are young, done to create uniform height and spread.

**Pollinator/s:** Bees, butterflies, moths, or hummingbirds that transfer pollen for fertilization from the male pollen-bearing organ (stamen) to the female organ (pistil).

**Pressure regulator:** An irrigation system component that reduces water pressure.

**Rainwater catchment system:** May include gutters, rainwater barrel/s, cistern/s, pump, piping, and valves that collect, store, and distribute rainwater to the landscape.

**Retrofit:** The process of keeping some elements, eliminating others, and rebuilding to fulfill new criteria. You might retrofit a landscape and irrigation system to be more water thrifty.

**Rough grade:** When soil is leveled and smoothed out by use of equipment, after construction is complete, but before the working of the soil and preparing to plant has commenced.

**Rhizome:** An underground horizontal stem that grows side shoots. Examples: canna, ginger, most irises.

**Rootball:** The network of roots and soil clinging to a plant when it is lifted out of the ground or pot.

**Runner:** A stem sprouting from a plant that roots itself as it goes. Also called a stolon.

**Soaker hose:** Attaches to a hosebib. A rubber hose that allows water to seep slowly out of the sides or flat tape with holes at intervals that allows water to slowly drip onto the soil.

**Shade:** A garden site that gets less than three hours of direct sunlight per day.

**Slow-release fertilizer:** A fertilizer that releases its nutrients slowly over time, meaning less-frequent applications are needed.

**Sod:** Pieces of turf, complete with soil, roots, and top growth, that are laid upon the ground to knit together to create a lawn area.

**Species:** A plant that's a variation or sub-group of a genus.

**Stormwater runoff:** Rain water or snow that has landed and flows off a surface.

**Silt:** A granular, mineral component of soil that's sized between that of smaller clay particles and larger sand particles.

**Soil test:** An analysis of a soil sample, most often to determine its level of nutrients and pH (acidity) reading.

**Succulent:** A group of plants that have fleshy leaves that hold water, often includes cactus plants.

**Sucker/ing:** Twiggy growth emerging from roots around the base of trees and tall shrubs. Suckering diverts energy from desirable tree growth and should be removed.

**Terrace:** A bench or shelf formed by a support wall, running parallel with a slope.

**Thinning:** In the context of pruning, it's the process of removing excess branches from woody plants to improve air flow, let more sunlight into the inner branches, and remove conflicts from branches that are rubbing one another.

**Topiary:** A specialized form of pruning and shearing to create geometric shapes, animals, and forms that are either free standing or within a wire form.

**Transplants:** Plants that are grown in one location and then moved to and replanted in another.

**Tuber:** Enlarged roots that send out shoots and roots from nodes along their surface. Examples: dahlia, cyclamen, perennial (tuberous) begonias.

**Turfgrass:** Short grasses that are mowed and used in lawns as opposed to ornamental grasses, which are left to grow as landscape plants.

**Turgidity:** State of plump or swollen plant parts that have high levels of moisture.

**Variegated:** The appearance of differently colored areas on plant leaves, usually white, yellow, or a brighter green.

**Vascular system:** Refers to the circulatory system of a plant, the xylem and phloem.

**Water-soluble fertilizer:** Plant fertilizer in a liquid form; some types need to be mixed with water, and some types are ready to use from the bottle.

**Wilt:** To become limp from lack of water, heat, root failure, pests, or disease.

**Wood chips:** Small pieces of wood made by cutting or chipping and used as mulch in the garden.

**Xeric, xeriphitic, xeriscape:** Refers to needing only a small amount of water to survive.

# INDEX

# Meet Diana Maranhao

Diana (Dee) Maranhao has been an active member of the horticulture and landscape industry for more than thirty-five years. Most of her professional career was spent in higher education, serving as a horticulture program manager, nursery production specialist, and finally as an educator specializing in xeriscape low-water-use landscaping, nursery production, and plant propagation. She developed and taught a program called "Xeriscape for the Classroom" and presented a monthly, full-day workshop to K–12 educators to give them the tools to teach water conservation gardening techniques to children in the classroom.

Upon retiring from her long tenure in education, Diana has served as horticulture editor and project editor for numerous educational texts, magazines, garden guides, and horticulture books. She has been a regularly featured garden columnist for more than ten years, authoring hundreds of gardening and horticulture articles for the public and the horticulture industry. This is Diana's second book; she is also the author of *Rocky Mountain Fruit & Vegetable Gardening* (Cool Springs Press, 2014).

Diana earned a degree in Ornamental Horticulture, completion certificates in Copyediting and Merchandising, and holds a life-time teaching credential from California, specializing in Ornamental Horticulture. She serves as Scholarship Chair for the Desert Green Foundation, Las Vegas, a non-profit group that presents a yearly educational conference for professionals to encourage continued learning in the landscape industry. She received the "2014 Professional of the Year" Award from *Southwest Trees & Turf Magazine* at the Desert Green XVIII Conference, Las Vegas, Nevada.

Diana and her husband, Steve, live and garden in southern Utah. Combining her professional background and education with the constant learning experience their gardens provide serves to encourage, teach, and inspire others to garden, and to do so with water conservation and sustainability of natural resources in mind.